THE SUNNY NIHILIST

THE
SUNNY
NIHILIST

A DECLARATION OF THE PLEASURE OF POINTLESSNESS

WENDY SYFRET

CHRONICLE PRISM

First published in the United States of America in 2022
by Chronicle Books LLC.
Originally published in the United Kingdom in 2021 by Souvenir Press.

Library of Congress Cataloging-in-Publication Data

Names: Syfret, Wendy, author.
Title: The sunny nihilist : a declaration of the pleasure of pointlessness
  / Wendy Syfret.
Identifiers: LCCN 2021037482 | ISBN 9781797215808 (hardback)
Subjects: LCSH: Happiness. | Nihilism.
Classification: LCC BF575.H27 S95 2022 | DDC 158--dc23
LC record available at https://lccn.loc.gov/2021037482

Manufactured in the United States of America.

Design by Pamela Geismar.
Typesetting by Happenstance Type-O-Rama. Typeset in Mercury Text
and Newcastle Basic.
Author photo on page 199 by Ben Thomson.

10 9 8 7 6 5 4 3 2 1

Chronicle books and gifts are available at special quantity discounts to
corporations, professional associations, literacy programs, and other
organizations. For details and discount information, please contact
our premiums department at corporatesales@chroniclebooks.com or
at 1-800-759-0190.

 CHRONICLE PRISM

Chronicle Prism is an imprint of Chronicle Books LLC,
680 Second Street, San Francisco, California 94107
www.chronicleprism.com

FOR MY FAMILY

CONTENTS

STOP TRYING TO MAKE   1
EVERYTHING A THING

A NEW KIND OF NIHILISM   19

THE MYTH OF MEANINGFUL WORK   59

FOLLOWING YOUR HEART   85
(INTO THE VOID)

LIFE AFTER GOD   107

THE DARK SIDE OF NIHILISM   129

SUNNY NIHILISM   149
FOR EVERYDAY LIFE

THE PLEASURE OF   173
POINTLESSNESS

ENDNOTES   181

ACKNOWLEDGMENTS   197

ABOUT THE AUTHOR   199

STOP TRYING TO MAKE EVERYTHING A THING

At the end of my street there is a sandwich board belonging to a store that, from what I can tell, sells candle-making ingredients. Each morning, it's updated with a motivational platitude: "Why carry the mountain when you could climb it?" "You don't have to see the whole staircase, just take the first step." "Be the hero of your own story." Once it helpfully advised passersby to "Do something great!" A few years ago, that sandwich board advertised discounts, opening hours, and more traditional candle-related news. But at some point, someone decided these stale practicalities were a waste of such cosmic space. The board needed to serve a more meaningful purpose. Now it regularly asks if today is the day you're going to change your life.

Selling candle-making ingredients has become secondary. Meaning itself is now the product.

This business isn't alone in its shift of perspective. In recent years the search for meaning has been upgraded from a private pursuit to a very marketable action. Today, the promise of, and search for, meaning has been grafted onto almost every part of our lives. A product, service, or experience is no longer judged simply on whether it's "good" or "bad," but whether or not it is, in some abstract way, "meaningful."

Maybe you don't have a sandwich board, maybe you have a podcast advertisement. The kind that talks about community, memory, nostalgia, and values for two minutes before revealing it's talking about mortgage insurance. Or a multinational confectionery company telling you that splitting a slab of chocolate is a meaningful act of multi-generational community engagement. Or an economically priced bodywash that's moisturizing and a radical representation of body positivity.

When the candle store began experimenting with its rebrand, I was working in digital media at a company where meaning's skyrocketing currency was becoming particularly apparent. One day I attended a meeting with some very smart copywriters as they brainstormed ways to communicate that a popular, delicious, and totally vacuous ice-cream brand *meant* something. The thinking was that if the consumer felt this ice cream was more than just ice cream, and embedded with some life-changing social or cultural value, they'd spend six dollars on it.

We kicked around a few ideas: Maybe people could share defining personal moments that conveniently involved this delicious snack? Or we could ask influencers to tie it back to their wellness habits? After over an hour of brainstorming increasingly lofty and wonkily noble reasons to not only buy reconstituted skim milk on a stick, but really *experience* it, one of my coworkers snapped, exclaiming: "It's just an ice cream! Just let it be an ice cream! Stop trying to make everything a *thing*!"

His suggestion wasn't adhered to. The ice cream, like the sandwich board, continued on its journey to find meaning. But since then, whenever faced with an overly earnest bit of marketing, I find myself wondering, "Why *does* everything have to be a thing? Why *can't* an ice cream just be an ice cream?"

PONDERING THE MEANING OF LIFE

This tendency to sew meaning into every piece of life isn't a radically new habit. As a kid I was conscious of the apparent importance of figuring out what it all *meant*. In Sunday school, Bible stories and crepe-paper crucifixes would regularly be interrupted by earnest adults leaning forward to ask, "What do *you* think Jesus's mission is for mankind? Why are we all here?" Gazing blankly back, I'd offer a well-worn generality like, "To be kind?"

The preoccupation with meaning continued when I got home and nestled into the warm cocoon of '90s kids'

TV. Between fart jokes and sibling pranks, *Arthur* examined identity, *Rocko's Modern Life* questioned the banality of suburban capitalism, *Hey Arnold!* considered the imprint of family trauma, and even *Rugrats*—a show about the exploits of babies—grappled with the endless expanse of death. *The Simpsons* basically made the interrogation of existence a subplot.

As the sun went down, the search for meaning followed me to bed. There, an exhausted parent would inevitably spend one of their precious free moments reading me a story featuring an interchangeable lineup of fish, insects, plants, animals, and kids who were all on their own personal, pint-sized quests for a meaningful life. Before falling asleep, the last words I'd hear would be rhyming couplets directing me towards a path of purpose.

Whether presented by an unpaid religious disciple, bathed in a soothing, Nickelodeon-orange glow, or embodied in an anthropomorphic tree, the implication was clear. The only way to fully enjoy and understand life was to spend every spare moment pondering the meaning of it.

The thing was, from what I could glean, it seemed pretty wild that I existed at all. The fact that my parents decided to have sex on some random day in 1987, at the instant the sperm and egg that made me were feeling particularly energized, allowing me to win the lottery of conception, already seemed significant. Add to that the luck of surviving birth and the near decade that followed. I wasn't sure why anyone needed to complicate things further; my very presence seemed complicated and miraculous enough.

But despite the impressive chaos surrounding us, parents, teachers, and even TV babies all seemed terrified by the idea of me facing a single meaningless moment. The irony was that despite their insistence otherwise, to me, the pointlessness of life kind of seemed central to its appeal.

When I couldn't sleep, or felt scared and overwhelmed, I'd think about the notes in human history that had to align for me to occur. I'd picture an unknowable mass of violent singularities, tangles of matter, energy, space, gravity, quarks, protons, and neutrons forming epochs and ecosystems over the past thirteen billion years or so. And attempt to comprehend all the brains that grew, teeth that shrank, and spines that straightened to form a string of faceless ancestors, stretching from the Pleistocene to me. I was a nervous kid, prone to silent crying sessions in school bathrooms, but that swirly mess of barely understood science and history became a go-to refuge. It made me, and my problems, feel very small. I understood that amid the tangle of that luminous turmoil nothing I did or didn't do would ever really matter. With context reaffirmed, I'd exit the bathroom stall feeling lighter, satisfied with the knowledge that my life was worthless, but I was lucky to have it.

TOO MUCH MEANING IS A TERRIBLE THING

Now, I'll concede that despite the firmness of those tween convictions, the search for meaning is of course not an inherently bad thing. Our quest for it has driven civilization forward. Quivering lovers swear that prior to their fateful meeting their lives were missing it. Weary heroes are propelled by it in times of exhausting crisis. Fallen villains interrogate it and find their blackened hearts lightened. Foundational concepts of community, ethics, logic, morality, consciousness, and equality were born from the investigation of it. The urge to wrestle with meaning has inspired great works of art, literature, and film. A lot of the time, we're better for it.

Meaning, perhaps more than anything else, offers comfort. In his 1946 book *Man's Search for Meaning*, Jewish psychiatrist and neurologist Viktor Frankl makes perhaps the most moving case for the value of meaning. Frankl, his first wife, and his parents were all interned in Nazi concentration camps during the Second World War. Throughout this time Frankl concluded that a sense of meaning and purpose would help him to maintain his sanity and ultimately survive. As German philosopher Friedrich Nietzsche (more on him later) said, and Frankl often quoted, "He who has a *why* to live for can bear almost any *how*."

Cognizant of that, I would suggest that meaning is most valuable when seen as an endpoint—a light on the horizon to guide and orient us in times of crisis or doubt. In which case, even if there is no final payoff, answer, or transcendent nirvana, the ongoing exploration of what we're all doing here (and to each other) is an honorable pursuit. Few people get to the end of a period of deep, honest, private contemplation and think, *Well, that was a waste of a decade.*

Problems arise when the promises and expectations tied to meaning begin to eclipse the concept itself. Which I would argue is exactly where we find ourselves (and our ice creams) today. Somewhere along the line, that noble, deeply personal, perhaps lifelong quest began to feel more urgent and commodified. The pursuit of meaning shifted from an epic journey to a scavenger hunt. It's not enough to try to locate purpose in love, family, work, or religion (although, readers beware, those areas hold their own traps). Now we're being asked to find meaning in everything we do. From our morning coffee to our weekend laundry load, each event or chore needs to be elevated into a clear-eyed statement about existence.

We wake up to push notifications from horoscope apps assigning us a cosmic narrative before we have a chance to turn off our alarms. Daily newsletters flood our inboxes, prescribing never-ending tasks and goals to meditate over and mark as complete. In the shower we listen to podcasts about making this day matter, then towel off and cram in a few minutes of mindful journaling about what we managed to meaningfully achieve the day before. When we exercise—a formerly (and pleasurably) mindless pursuit— we cue up playlists on slick apps designed to interrupt our solitude with a voice telling us what this exorcism of calories really means. And how with every step we're remaking ourselves and darting towards some unspecified new life that's only another 1.5 miles away.

I'd like to say that my Happy Meal–sized philosophical epiphanies buffered me from all that. For a while, my dedication to meaninglessness held steady, ruining many Sunday school classes, philosophy lectures, and stoner conversations along the way. Whenever I felt sorry for myself or lost, I'd return to the swirling mass of random occurrences that had resulted in my birth and think, *Well, at least that all worked out.* My smallness, in the world and my own mind, offered a strange sense of peace. But, as it turns out, not even a lifelong devotee of pointlessness is able to totally avoid the deadly and decadent trap of meaning.

THE DANGERS OF INSTANT ENLIGHTENMENT

My entanglement in the rising commercial value of meaning moved from perplexing to toxic when I was working in that digital media job during the 2010s. Journalism is hard and expensive, and unfortunately the most deeply thought out, well-researched, actually purposeful content often doesn't get read. It's a painful reality for editors and writers who are pulled between their dedication to the public good and the managers standing over them asking if anything will "go viral" that week. But, as it turns out, there is an easy workaround embedded in our brains' aforementioned desire for enlightenment and a sense of purpose.

It's human to want to understand what all *this* actually means. It's also a lot of work. In the past writers and philosophers dedicated their lives to answering life's big questions. Henry David Thoreau spent years living mostly alone in the woods while writing *Walden*, his critique of the West's relationship with consumerism and the destruction of nature. Epicurus founded The Garden, a literal microsociety where his followers lived together in total pursuit of understanding and achieving happiness. Editors don't have that kind of time. But if you can figure out how to offer the valuable feeling of introspection and reward in, say, a four-minute read with a good Instagram-deliverable strategy, it's a much easier and more economic sell.

This is one of the reasons that in the past decade, you've probably observed as the internet's limitless expanse of digital space is colonized by masturbatory first-person narratives blindly assigning meaning to every animal, vegetable, and mineral within a quarter mile radius of a writer's desk. Recently a friend shared an article about what "sitting" really means. Before I could reply in exasperation, I remembered that I have written stagnant explorations on such enriching topics as exclamation marks, the class implications of soda choices, and what Skeet Ulrich's Instagram says about intergenerational internet use.

These wafer-thin examinations drive clicks, audience growth, ad sales, and social shares. Which is how they made their way onto the intellectual assembly line, and former explorations of meaning that once took years were replaced by 800-word hot takes that had to be filed before the newsletter went out at lunch.

To this day I can look at a half-dead potted plant and work out a way to argue that it's a statement about post-internet morality, or our pursuit of peace in an urban setting, or the decaying perennial adolescence so many of us feel trapped in. Sure, it's not a skill that greatly benefits the human race, but it is a survival adaptation for a system and culture where meaning has become twisted into a form of currency that everyone is very keen to cash in on.

Our growing love of this fast-acting enlightenment is easy to make fun of. But it's also deeply understandable. While I've been skeptical since birth of taking things too seriously, there is no doubt that some things should be deeply interrogated. Just because your choice of luxury frozen dessert doesn't matter isn't to say that nothing else does. As Frankl showed, meaning has the capacity to make the pain and confusion of life a little easier to bear.

I was writing this book as the 2020 Black Lives Matter protests erupted around the world, and issues of race, violence, and power began to be unpacked and disseminated on a scale most of us had never witnessed in our lifetime. Every person, every platform, every corporation (some better than others) became obsessed with trying to understand not just the news, but how these events informed and influenced all aspects of public and private life. It was a period when there was huge value in considering the meaning behind all things: What systems contributed to the life I have? How have I been helped while others have been hindered? How do my daily choices, small and large, contribute to the health and safety of people I may never even meet?

That kind of interrogation is rewarding, transformative, and has a huge capacity for good. It's also intensely stressful and often painful. It rewrites history, and displaces us in our own understanding of morality, fairness, and worth. Which is why, outside of the world-altering news moments that dominate social and traditional media and demand our attention, most of us avoid it. In its place, we prefer an easier form of evaluation, one built around the thing that is most familiar: ourselves.

Trying to assign extreme value to the most pointless parts of our lives feels great at first. That second cookie you're eating is a personal stand against misogynistic beauty standards. Posting a flattering photo of yourself to Instagram is an act of empowerment. Sleeping in is an affront to capitalist culture. Your sixth glass of wine and eventual hangover are a fuck you to the cult of productivity. Doing nothing at all can quickly start to feel very important. But spend too much time in this space and things begin to distort: Petty grievances become life-changing proceedings; we expand to take up space in our own brains that we probably don't deserve.

Over time, innocuous concepts like meaning and purpose turn corrosive as all that obsessive thought, fixation, and study of our own minds and lives fails to return any sense of relief or clarity. In fact, it starts making a lot of us feel worse.

SEARCHING FOR RELIEF

In my own life, I began to notice that as I abandoned my meditative childhood commitment to pointlessness, and participated in this hedonistic worship of purpose, things started to spiral. With meditation apps telling me today was *the* day, podcast hosts assuring me I was *the one,* and that damn sandwich board telling me this was *the* moment, I started to view my world from a new, warped perspective.

As meaning increasingly became the metric, I sought and assigned it to areas of my life that until a few years ago I would barely have given a second thought. Anything I wasn't able to immediately assign a point was deemed a waste of time and energy. I became obsessed with locating a reason in everything I did—worrying about how I spent my time, feeling guilty if I wasn't constantly involved in "meaningful" pursuits.

In many ways, my life during this period was going pretty well. I had a "cool" job that I liked being asked about at parties, a nice partner, a cute apartment, and enough money to have enabled a preference for cloudy wine that tastes like sand. But rather than taking a breath, glancing around and considering how pleasant it all was, I was consumed by what it all *meant.*

The thing about meaning is that it's most valuable when in short supply, and best served in a sea of pointlessness. In the past you might have hoped to have had a handful of meaningful things in your life: a partner, a hobby, a social cause, even a job. They'd take up a lot of time, but be surrounded by other, non-meaningful (and hence less consuming) subjects. Remove the pointlessness, and the pressure starts to build, leaving you constantly wondering: What's the point, the aim, the benefit, the end goal of all this? What's it adding to my life, my being, my identity? When those questions can't be answered, any act (however pleasant) can start to feel like a waste of time.

This experience wasn't entirely internal. At work I noticed my performance was no longer judged on the completion and quality of tasks, but rather held up to an existential framework of what it all *meant*. Most of the time no one cared very much if the work was actually valuable or making the world a better place, rather that it fit into the haphazard narrative of purpose we'd all sleep-walked into.

The language of fast-acting meaning and purpose is conspicuously pliable: It can be delivered via an ice-cream ad, a sandwich board, or a boss. Everyone embraces it, believing it's about them, when really it's about no one and nothing. This bottomless hunger for easy-access meaning consumes huge amounts of our time and attention, but offers nothing more than a passing feeling that we're doing something worthwhile. The problem is, once you start believing in all this, it's hard to stop.

Once I'd been a child immune to the perpetual call of meaning. I took pleasure in feeling small in a world so huge and complex that my own presence seemed little more than a lucky fluke. But over time I reluctantly transformed into the kind of adult that had previously perplexed me: a creature terrified by the possibility of a meaningless moment.

I mostly enjoyed my job but sometimes found it frustrating or boring. In the context of human history, that is not a terrible problem to have. But when I sat at my desk, wondering what the point of every email, interaction, and meeting was, I'd become terrified that I was wasting my life. Rather than recognize my employment as a pathway to feeding and clothing myself that didn't require me to stand too much, it contorted into an ideogram of my seemingly wasted life and the inevitability of death dragging its way across the office's polished concrete floor.

When I unwound with my partner after a day of existential dread, he sometimes wasn't able to completely comprehend my unique emotional chaos. Rather than feel briefly disconnected from someone I knew I loved deeply, I'd spiral over the nature of true love and the tragedy of not accomplishing a perfect soul bond.

On Sunday nights, reviewing the weekend, all I could see was what I didn't do, didn't achieve. Ordinary days were marked down as dismal failures. As if waking up, feeding myself, spending time with other humans, and generally not doing catastrophic harm was something to be deeply ashamed of. If I were to pause and map out the parameters of a "good life," I'd find them encircling me. But even when I tried to remind myself of this, everything still felt empty. Rather than bringing me peace and fulfillment, grafting meaning onto all my actions, achievements, and victories left them feeling oddly tarnished. Nothing could ever live up to the esoteric hype I compulsively placed on it. It was a lot. As that noisy anxiety began to swell inside me, I once again took up silently crying in bathroom stalls. When I did this as a kid, I'd comforted myself with the reminder that my problems (and I) didn't really matter. Facing my own smallness was a comfort. Now, I was overwhelmed by the apparent, albeit totally unexplained, importance of every single action. Sometimes I'd stare dead-eyed into the mirror, muttering, "This isn't the whole world, this isn't the whole world," over and over like it was an incantation holding the roof up. Focusing on meaning hadn't expanded my mind; it had resulted in a self-obsession so complete I needed to literally remind myself I wasn't *actually* the physical center of the universe.

I tried to speak to others about this inverted existential dread. And while we couldn't always explain it, there were a lot of us laboring under the same scramble of purpose, pain, stress, and fast-acting fulfillment. It congealed in our bodies, introducing a creeping malaise of dissatisfaction. But investigating the mounting feeling only returned the same cyclical advice: To feel whole, we just needed to keep searching for the elusive point to our lives. Once located— through some combination of therapy, deep breathing, good lighting, motivational podcasts, imported foods, and stretching in humid rooms—we'd be relieved. Our lives would be stamped "meaningful."

Obviously, that point never emerged. The only thing I discovered was if you clench your jaw hard enough, your teeth will start to crack. Instead, all the pressure, confusion, fear, and exhaustion finally came to a head late one night while I was walking home from work. A few blocks from my home I began to feel lightheaded. The growing tension inside me seemed to be finally cutting off airflow.

Doubled over, struggling to take a full breath, my heart racing, everything felt like such a *thing*. There was no part of my life I hadn't laden down with the heavy task of having a point. It all felt so impossibly important. There was no escape. No quiet, pointless place I could picture for a second to catch my breath. I'd hijacked every crevice of reality and crammed it full of expectations, significance, and let's face it, myself. Slowly, over years, I'd rewritten my own existence, spinning an egocentric delusion where my mundane life in a medium-sized city at the edge of the world felt like it was of biblical consequence.

Then it hit me. A realization rang out so clearly that another person might wonder if it was divine intervention. "Who cares, one day I'll be dead and no one will remember me anyway."

The sense of relief was immediate. Straightening up I looked at the sky and thought, *I'm just a chunk of meat hurtling through space on a rock. Futile and meaningless.* My chest relaxed, my lungs inflated, for the first time in years the mist cleared. I thought of everything I cared about, stressed over, lay awake at night worrying for, and saw it for what it was—ultimately pointless. In a hundred years no one would give a shit about my job. No one would give a shit about me.

I was immediately transported back to my eight-year-old self. My brain felt clear and my body loose. I thought about the mass of matter, the billions of years, the unknowable bodies that had carried me to this space, and how I'd be washed away in the continually crashing wave of time and memory. The way I figured it, maybe a few people per generation are remembered for anything. And even then, maybe for a few hundred years if they're lucky. Eventually, the greatest achievements, the highest minds, the most meaningful moments are forgotten. And even if I did somehow manage to achieve anything of note, to be entangled in the public consciousness for a generation or two, I wouldn't be around to enjoy it.

When I got home that night my dog greeted me at the door as usual. Reaching down to pick her up, I stared at her little face and felt her chicken carcass of a body wiggling between my hands. "Stevie, in the course of human history, we're probably equally valuable to the planet." Viewed over a billion years, her daily schedule of finding sleeping spots of varying temperatures wasn't more or less noble than anything I'd ever do. Someday we'd both die, be buried or cremated, and return to an indistinguishable mineral state.

Everything was futile. Nothing meant anything or mattered. Just like that, my life was handed back to me. Or rather, the life I had as an eight-year-old. It was the most comforting realization of my life. I'd discovered a sunnier side of nihilism.

A NEW KIND
OF NIHILISM

I t is not an overstatement to say that nihilism has an
image problem. When the term comes up we tend
to picture grumpy Europeans, shrouded in black coats,
beards, and bad moods. Mention you're a nihilist and you'll
notice the air around you chill, eyes glaze over, and conversation partners melt away. During the writing of this book
people would often ask why I'd want to dedicate so much
of my time to exploring such a miserable subject. When
I started making my case that the philosophy didn't fully
deserve its icy reputation, that in fact nihilism could offer
an uplifting and valuable outlook, they'd nod for a few
moments before eventually asking: "So what actually *is*
nihilism?"

Nihilism is one of those terms that everyone uses very freely, often without fully understanding what it means. It's subbed in for "negative" or "depressing," a perennial indicator of a bad vibe. So before we can examine our changing relationship to the concept—or attempt to recondition our understanding of it—we need to go back to how nihilism has traditionally been perceived and understood.

To be fair, it's understandable that so many people struggle with the concept: It is purposely vacant. Even the word "nihilism" is an abyss. It comes from the Latin *nihil*, or nothing. In the simplest terms, that's what it's about: emptiness, a void. Nihilists (or at least the stereotype of them) believe meaning, values, and purpose don't inherently exist. That they're human-made constructs we willingly assemble to constrain and comfort ourselves. Systems around morality, decency, and goodness are therefore not somehow baked into the fabric of life and existence, as inherent as air or gravity. Rather they are simply ideas that we have chosen to etch into our own collective reality.

By that thinking, some could argue (and they do) that our ties to these values are also temporal. If nothing matters, you have no purpose, and if morality is a fantasy, then what's the point of anything? Why get out of bed in the morning? Or earn money? Or look after yourself? Or make polite yet agonizing small talk with your neighbors? Or attempt to follow any social guidelines around goodness, if, after all, "goodness" doesn't exist? It's not a coincidence that the root *nihil* also appears in the verb "annihilate."

When you begin thinking like that, things have the potential to unravel pretty fast.

Breaking down further the most common reading of nihilism, it's often talked about within three general categories: political nihilism, ethical (or moral) nihilism, and existential nihilism. Depending on who you ask, the specifics of these vary. But to make sure we're all basically on the same page, let's condense them to the following handful that speak to most of our lives and experiences.

Historically, political nihilism has arguably cast the longest shadow, reaching beyond theoretical discussion and directly influencing real-world events. Political nihilism rejects political, social, and religious systems, structures, and authority. It's frequently associated with the Russian anarchists of the nineteenth century who took issue with the sweeping powers afforded to the church and monarchy, and how constructs of authority and class allowed ordinary people to be exploited by the aristocracy. This period of rampant nihilism was punctuated by the assassination of Tsar Alexander II in 1881, a PR crisis that still hangs over the philosophy today.

While the violence committed by some political nihilists is chilling, the questions political nihilism asks about how and why accepted power structures are able to justify one group's terrorizing of another are valid. In recent years we've all witnessed the urgent need to reform and reject beliefs that once existed unchallenged in the mainstream. In particular this can be observed in the Black Lives Matter protesters' calls to abolish and defund police, empty prisons, and overhaul the bail systems. These activists look at the current way we live, designate authority, and define safety, and argue: This clearly isn't working. Rather than blindly following these ideas of law and order, they interrogate the history that brought us to this place, questioning myths we tell ourselves about the role of the police in our communities. Ultimately, these protesters and activists aren't out to destroy neighborhoods or welcome an era of chaos. They're urging people to step back and ask: Why do we live this way? Why do we support structures that don't work, that we don't believe in, just because they're seen as the way to do things? How can we do better?

This crosses closely into ethical or moral nihilism—which, outside of revolutions, has historically also inspired a lot of angst among non-prescribers—and rejects absolute moral or ethical values. It argues that even our most basic ideas of good and evil are constructs of context, history, and social conditioning. Following this thinking, one could ask: How can others judge my behavior as immoral if morality is an illusion?

If you've ever tumbled into alt-right YouTube, Reddit, and podcast holes you'll have likely witnessed moral nihilism reigning supreme. In these spaces, supporters—who are often, but not always, white men—use the outlines of nihilism to endlessly unpack morality and the existence of racism, sexism, antisemitism, and a rainbow of other bigotries. Chances are you found the whole experience unpleasant, but try not to let it inform your whole experience of these ideas.

For all the different ways to slice and dice it, most of these varied interpretations ultimately level up to existential nihilism: the all-encompassing mother theory that breezes past variations and declares simply that life itself is meaningless. Everything we do, or don't do, is irrelevant, nothing is building to anything, we're not being guided by some cosmic force. Every moment of love, pain, joy, tribulation ever experienced by a human is random and senseless.

Existential nihilism, and the overwhelming sense of smallness that comes from thinking like this, often leads to a much-discussed sense of existential dread. That being the familiar flood of terror you have undoubtedly felt lying awake at 2 A.M., wondering: *What's the point of any of this?*

Viewed all laid out like that, it's not hard to see why people shudder at nihilism and nihilists. Throughout modern history, nihilism hasn't been presented as the most appealing product. Meaning offers reason, comfort, connection. It's a tough habit to ask people to kick. What is life without it?

NIHILISM'S PR PROBLEM

In 2018, someone in Australia (where I live) started putting needles in supermarket strawberries. To be clear, not in the baskets, but carefully, invisibly, embedded in the fruit itself. It was like that urban legend of razor blades being embedded in children's Halloween candy, except it was real. People around the country reported biting into pieces of their favorite fruit and having a needle wedge in their mouths. Some were hospitalized after swallowing them. It became international news and badly hurt the Australian fruit industry. Farmers and supermarkets began dumping tons and tons of product. Strawberries disappeared from menus and shoppers were told to toss any they'd already bought. The hashtag #smashastrawb trended, as everyone began obsessively cutting and crushing all fruit before consuming. The Queensland government (the warm northern state where much of the country's fruit is grown) announced a $1 million AUD assistance package for the strawberry industry.

Copycat incidents appeared to emerge, as needles were found in bananas and apples too. It was reported that there were over a hundred cases of needles being found in fruit, but it became difficult to distinguish between hoaxes and unsubstantiated internet claims. People were terrorized by the fear of not only biting into a needle—an act so uniquely disturbing that it feels like it belongs in a *Saw* movie, not a news bulletin—but also at the reality that someone in their community could do something so cruel. As it was unclear if the sabotage was occurring during harvesting, packing, or at the stores themselves, anyone could have been the morally vacant perpetrator.

At the time, one thought kept ringing through my head: The line between order and chaos is so fine. Prior to 2018, the thought of someone putting a needle into a strawberry probably hadn't occurred to most people.

You've likely obliviously bitten into thousands of pieces of fruit (and obviously other foods you didn't grow or prepare yourself) without a second of hesitation. But consider for a moment the last thing you ate, all the countless hands it passed through that you will never know or be able to account for. Without thinking about it, you blindly and implicitly trusted that each of those anonymous individuals had your best interests in mind. You are able to wake up each day, pour a bowl of cereal, buy a take-out coffee, or pick up a prepackaged sandwich, and not be crushed by thoughts of the endless opportunities for someone to harm you, because you've internalized and projected a silent but agreed-upon code of conduct that humans, moving through their days, won't hurt each other at random.

But why not? Obviously, no one wants to be arrested and humiliated for an act as cowardly and cruel as sticking a needle in a strawberry, but it's also a covert move. You could easily imagine no one would ever catch you if you did it.

The original perpetrator was eventually revealed to be a disgruntled farm supervisor who acted out of spite. Police alleged that she felt mistreated by her colleagues. Two years after the events took place, she was charged with six counts of "contamination of goods to cause economic loss." Police have noted that of the 230 needle incidents reported around the country, the remainder are unresolved. That means there are still people walking around, speaking to their family, picking their kids up, making dinner, who decided—for reasons we'll never know—to perform a simple act to maim and traumatize a stranger. People you would probably never suspect because you believe a shared morality system protects you. Two hundred and thirty cases showed that it is an easily pierced fantasy.

That incident still haunts the country. People bring it up regularly whenever fruit is bought or served. We inspect our food and slice into it before popping it into our mouths, not because we're consciously afraid of needles (although I still cut my fruit), but because we're afraid of how easily the order that we've built our sanity around can be disrupted. That chaos is what terrifies people about nihilism. If one person diverging from a moral system can terrorize a country, what would happen if we all rejected it?

Humans need meaning, not just to feel safe, but to literally live. In his book *The Birth and Death of Meaning*, American cultural anthropologist Ernest Becker writes: "Anthropologists have long known that when a tribe of people loses the feeling that their way of life is worthwhile, they may stop reproducing, or in large numbers simply lie down and die beside streams full of fish."

Meaning offers moral guidance, comfort, and connection. Nihilism, often, counters with anarchism, depression, and complete psychological destruction.

Chatting about this book with my mom one afternoon, I took her through some of the ideas I was exploring: that we overinvest in meaning, refuse to question it, and in turn are oppressed as much as comforted by it. She nodded politely as I wondered if we only believe in things because they make us feel safe and valuable, and privately know we have invested so much in them that to reject them now would be shattering. When I'd finished, she cleared away our teacups and answered, "That all sounds great, as long as you don't actually believe it."

I was a bit thrown, replying, "What do you mean I don't believe it? I'm writing a book arguing for it."

Her face dropped. "Oh, Wends, but it's so depressing to think like that."

This widely held distaste for nihilism isn't totally undeserved or built off a misunderstanding of the subject. It has repeatedly become tangled in the darkest parts of human history and behavior. Helmut Thielicke, a German theologian, has suggested that the inherent amorality of nihilism led to the rise of fascism and the Nazi party in 1930s Germany. Those ties exist to this day, evolving into an uneasy relationship between nihilism and the alt-right.

To understand how a purposely empty way of viewing the world has become filled with such darkness, it pays to spend some time with Friedrich Nietzsche, the German philosopher and cultural critic who has become the poster boy for nihilism.

Nietzsche hated systems and fixed moral principles; he saw no objective order to life beyond what we give it. Many choose to fixate on this rejection of traditional belief systems and understanding of meaning. Yes, Nietzsche felt that moral and social conventions stifled individual thought and reason, but he didn't say we should destroy them for the sake of it—rather that we should think for ourselves, look at our own lives, and confront the social and moral forces pressing down on us.

As with so many brilliant people, Nietzsche's life was turbulent and productive. In 1869, at the age of twenty-four, he was made a professor in classical philology at the University of Basel. He was the youngest professor in the university's 400-year history. A few years later, at twenty-seven, he published the first of his iconic works, *The Birth of Tragedy*. Sadly, Nietzsche was stalked by mental and physical illness. After a decade at the university he resigned due to health problems. The next ten years saw the completion of his most famous and defining writings, including *The Gay Science, Thus Spoke Zarathustra, On the Genealogy of Morality*, and *Twilight of the Idols*. Approaching the turn of the century, at the age of forty-four he suffered a mental breakdown and spent the rest of his life being cared for by his mother and his sister, Elisabeth Förster-Nietzsche. By the end of his life, following multiple strokes, he was unable to talk. He died in 1900, never fully witnessing how his thinking would come to influence the twentieth century.

In his final years Nietzsche was unable to continue producing the work that had made him famous. After his death, works by Nietzsche continued to be disseminated into the culture, delivered via his sister Elisabeth, who took control of his archives and posthumous publishing. It's here that we see a fracture in how his ideas were presented and directed.

Elisabeth was a committed Nazi. In a surreal collision of history, in 1887 she and her husband Bernhard founded

Nueva Germania: the infamous "Aryan" colony in Paraguay. They, along with fourteen other "racially pure" German families, planned to establish what Simon Romero, writing for the *New York Times*, described as "a colony from which an advance contingent of Aryans could forge a claim to the entire South American continent." Their mission was the "purification and rebirth of the human race."

The whole experiment was a mess. The group was ravaged by disease, infighting, crop failures, and Elisabeth and Bernhard's megalomania. The plan fell apart within two years, the couple returned home, and Bernhard took his own life in 1889. After his death, Elisabeth turned her full attention to establishing a Nietzsche archive.

Usually, protecting and promoting the legacy of an ailing genius is noble work, but Elisabeth used it as a chance to edit and manipulate Nietzsche's writing to fit her own racist agenda.

Nietzsche was a product of his time, and in the late nineteenth century, Germany was a deeply antisemitic society, but Nietzsche's writing suggests he didn't subscribe to this thinking. In her Nietzsche biography *I Am Dynamite!*, Sue Prideaux notes that he was interested in man as "an individual, rather than man as a herd animal." Elaborating for the *Guardian,* she added, "Growing up in Bismarck's reich, there were three things Nietzsche hated: the big state, nationalism, and antisemitism." This was a man who rejected all systems, and wrote that he didn't want to engage with anyone with a "share in the mendacious race swindle."

In fact, Michael F. Duffy and Willard Mittelman write in their paper "Nietzsche's Attitudes Toward the Jews" that he "decried the increasing nationalism of European countries and suggests that it is this nationalism which foments antisemitic thinking." Despite being anti all religions, Nietzsche admitted to admiring the "enlightenment and intellectual independence" of the Jewish individuals in his life. The end of Nietzsche's intense friendship with composer Richard Wagner was partially due to the latter's antisemitism and German nationalism (Wagner and Elisabeth remained chummy).

But this was all redacted in Elisabeth's editing and arranging of Nietzsche's unpublished content. Trawling his archive, she cut and pasted his work and combined it with her own interpretations, publishing a subjective biography and *The Will to Power,* a manipulated collection of Nietzsche's writings. *The Will to Power* was read widely in Nazi Germany. When Elisabeth died in 1935, Hitler attended her funeral.

Eighty-five years after his sister's death, nihilism and Nietzsche are still regularly tied to some of the most brutal and bleak expressions of human reason possible (more about that later). The irony is that despite being the face of it, and inspiring a lot of (anarchistic) downers, Nietzsche didn't believe anyone should enfold themselves in nihilism full-time. Rather, he saw it as a state to pass through on the way to something else. When he rejected systems and prescribed ideas of reason and morality, it wasn't because he didn't think they should exist, but rather that they should be subjects we explore for ourselves.

Additionally, as a critic of organized religion (seriously, I can't stress how anti-religion he was), Nietzsche was concerned over how existing ideas of reason and morality were fixated on what's next. He didn't believe this life, and our good behavior in it, should be driven by ideas of God or a long-term plan to get into some preferable afterlife—or a "true world," as this heaven-like state was often referred to. Viewed like that, he worried existence was undervalued, treated as a mere dress rehearsal, something to get through and leave behind. Nietzsche said that this allows individuals to take the stance of "judge of the world who in the end places existence itself upon his scales and finds it wanting."

He worried that this approach encouraged apathy and disconnection, and removed personal responsibility. It allowed a person to witness suffering and immediately comfort themselves with the belief it would be addressed in the next life. But if you reject meaning, placing you squarely in the reality of the present moment, accepting there is no cosmic divination or kindness, you are left with the responsibility of acting now. You can't expect the universe to course correct later.

Nietzsche saw nihilism and his work as a way to help us become ourselves. He didn't mock meaning; he understood its power and didn't want it to be wielded blindly or accepted passively. He was weary of systems that offered convenient answers and prevented us from asking, *Why do we live like this? Why is power structured in this way? Does this align with what I truly believe? Have I established my own ideas of good and evil?*

In *The Gay Science* he wrote: "Gradually, man has become a fantastic animal that has to fulfill one more condition of existence than any other animal: man has to believe, to know, from time to time why he exists; his race cannot flourish without a periodic trust in life—without faith in reason in life." Nietzsche didn't die a nihilist. He used it as a lens to look more critically at his life and himself.

It's this reading of nihilism that I think about when considering an alternative impression of a life without meaning. Sunny nihilism breaks away from the previous fixation on destruction by viewing pointlessness as a chance to breathe and think. Ultimately serving as a blank page, a chance to enjoy the moment, the present, the chaos, and the luck of being alive at all.

Despite Nietzsche's efforts to present nihilism as a textured and kinetic theory, a hundred years after his death the stereotypes we hold about nihilists still feel firmly rooted in the past. But the evolving presence of sunny nihilism is comfortably alive and well today. In fact, I'd argue it's more popular than ever.

NIHILISM FOR THE TWENTY-FIRST CENTURY

When I first began thinking about this book, I became aware of seeing nihilism everywhere. Yes, I was reading and talking about it a lot, but the most pervasive and evocative examples weren't found in lectures or articles. Rather it was subtly but deeply embedded in the shifting pop and internet culture I consumed every day.

Nihilism has a way of taking the shape of what we fear most at any given moment. It's tricky and adaptive, evolving to reflect each year's changing preoccupations and concerns. In the nineteenth and twentieth centuries people looked at nihilism and saw the shadow of modernity: during a time where science had displaced God in minds and hearts, it spoke to the anxiety of what a post-religious world would look like. Critics worried that its embrace of nothingness could refract and lead to fascism, violence, and a total devolution of personal and social morality.

Exploring nihilism today, you spot a new uneasiness. It lurks in our discussion of climate change, neoliberalism, the failings of capitalism, and the malaise of loneliness and disconnection we usually blame on the internet. But in recent years, it's bled in from the fringes to inform much of millennial and Gen Z's identity, taste, humor, and attitudes. In place of nineteenth-century philosophers scribbling by candlelight we have teens on TikTok jokingly begging the universe to kill them, meme accounts lol-ing about the meaninglessness of life, the dead-eyed and self-medicated heroine of *My Year of Rest and Relaxation*, and the proudly bleak music of Billie Eilish and Lana Del Rey.

In the past few years I've seen one article written again and again by numerous journalists across multiple publications. Sometimes it looks at Twitter or Instagram, sometimes at Netflix and YouTube. More recently, it has been fixated on TikTok. By the time you read this it will probably have another focal point—although I'd bet it's still asking the same question: Why is millennial and Gen Z content so dark and weird?

I don't blame people for asking. Personally, I have been noticing changes in what makes me laugh for a while. Like many people who grew up online, carefully tending to a digital facsimile of myself, I spend a lot of time scrolling through Instagram, DMing memes to my friends, and tagging people under posts while simply writing "us." Day to day I consider myself a pretty well-adjusted, happy-ish human, whose conversations generally hover around news, banal gossip, and things I have just eaten or plan to eat soon. But if you were to create a map of my life through the memes, articles, accounts, and videos I like and share, you'd probably think something more problematic was going on.

Looking at my social media (I personally stick mostly to Twitter and Instagram, and dip into TikTok only occasionally), most of the accounts I follow are a lumpy mash of humor, politics, news, activism, art, and witty, snappily written declarations of crushing melancholy. I scroll through posts and am met with disembodied screen grabs from reality TV shows, quotes from philosophers and social theorists, calls to dismantle capitalism, and many, many variations of jokes that basically equate to "I feel very anxious and bad all the time."

Cat Cohen, a musical comedian (I promise it's better than it sounds), uploads a video of herself to Twitter rehearsing a song about "the void." In it she sings about how the hole inside her is "annoying" so she tries to fill it with "lots of melted cheese–based products, lots and lots of gin and tonics, sex with people who say things like 'howdy,' SOS, everything they make at Zara, photos where they read your aura, endless apps about astrology." The comments below are filled with laughing and fire emojis; people call it their theme song. I DM it to a friend, writing "she gets it."

Further down my feed someone shares a screenshot from *BoJack Horseman*, a cartoon that follows a clutch of humans and anthropomorphic animals as they navigate Hollywood, fame, and their own cycles of ambition and destruction. In it, Mr. Peanutbutter, a lovable and dimwitted Labrador who is also a successful TV actor, consoles his ex-wife by tenderly reminding her, "The universe is a cruel, uncaring void. The key to being happy isn't a search for meaning. It's to just keep yourself busy with unimportant nonsense, and eventually, you'll be dead." The scene is played for laughs, and comments below it repeat the multiple laugh/crying emojis.

Over on TikTok, a peppy Pilates instructor reminds her followers that no matter how much water they drink, sleep they get, or exercise they do they're still going to die one day. Someone in the comments asks where she got her star-spangled water bottle from.

Early on during the 2020 COVID-19 outbreak, lots of people were retweeting a news article about Japanese theme parks banning screaming. Instead, they asked guests to "Please scream inside your heart." Almost everyone captioned it with variations of "Way ahead of you."

Everything feels very serious, but also like a total joke.

Perhaps the most common, or at least strikingly illuminating strain of dark humor belongs to the waves of regular, seemingly unremarkable internet inhabitants casually wishing for death or begging famous people on Twitter to kill and maim them. It's hard, writing this sentence, in my home, with my boyfriend vacuuming in the next room, to express why this is funny and relatable, but it is. I often offhandedly request a loved one to murder me, or catch myself nonchalantly declaring that I wish some gentle celebrity would slowly crush me to death. I wish for this obliteration in the same way a few years ago I might have daydreamed about what it would be like to visit a farmers' market with them.

In her 2019 *New Yorker* article "Love, Death, and Begging for Celebrities to Kill You," Jia Tolentino wondered about the phenomenon. She suggested it wasn't only a reflection of fandom, but "that we're craving unmediated connection so desperately that we would accept it in the form of murder. It's also possible that we simply want to die." Twitter user @alwayssaddaily, who had tweeted about wanting to be run over, reflected to her on the sense of pointlessness that connects so much of this content: "Life is becoming increasingly redundant, which makes me iterate these thoughts out loud to myself—hit me with a car, fucking kill me—for psychological satisfaction."

Taking on the same phenomenon in an article with the incredible title "Why Does Everyone Want Their Crushes to Run Them Over?" on *The Cut* a few months earlier, Gabriella Paiella wondered if "the joke's popularity may also have to do with the fact that we're living during a time when we're constantly being reminded that the Earth is going to be virtually uninhabitable by the end of the century, that capitalism is wholly unsustainable, and that we're just one push of a button away from perishing in a nuclear war." In light of all that she concludes that "A breathless 'run me over' matches our current fatalistic mood."

Nihilism's appearance in pop culture isn't a new occurrence. In the '80s, the movies *Thief*, *Less than Zero*, and *Heathers* all presented characters who embraced the void and reveled in a rejection of traditional morality and values. The '90s were rife with pop-nihilists too: The Coen brothers, Harmony Korine, Larry Clark, and Quentin Tarantino all made films that housed dangerous and violent nihilists. But their appearances felt more fleeting and novel. Nihilists were an archetype marking evil or desperation. They're villains in *The Big Lebowski* and *Heathers*, and symbols of cultural decay in *Pulp Fiction*.

But the more recent pop-nihilists have moved away from these overly dramatic bogeymen. Their actions feel less like moral warnings than rational responses to the current state of the world.

Harmony Korine has been making movies about nihilism since the beginning of his career. Much of his earlier work explores the disillusionment of young misfits living outside of the systems that usually contain and define modern life in the United States. His (often teen) characters gaze at the adult world as it fast approaches them, declare it corrupt and worthless, and embrace chaos and annihilation as an alternative. Speaking to the *Guardian* in 2016 about his work, he said: "I want to do extreme damage. I want to be disruptive, I don't care about the flow and I don't want to go with it."

Korine is now approaching fifty and recognized as a Gen X icon, but his movies (especially 2012's *Spring Breakers*) have become sacred objects to many people born years after his early, career-defining, and hugely controversial films were released. *Spring Breakers* updates his aforementioned nihilist themes for the new millennium as it follows a gang of pretty college students partially made up of former Disney stars. The group is dead set on traveling to Florida for spring break. Early in the film they gleefully rob a restaurant to finance their trip. It's the first of many crimes they commit in an escalating whirl of drugs, partying, sex, and a dedication to an absolute good time. The central characters are driven by consumption and empty of guilt or morality. No lessons are learned or taught. Along the way they encounter more traditional career criminals and leave them trembling in their wake.

Reviewing *Spring Breakers* for the *New York Times*, Manohla Dargis explained that the movie took the pursuit of happiness "to nihilistic extremes—but [Korine] turns his exploration into such a gonzo, outrageously funny party that it takes a while to appreciate that this is more of a horror film than a comedy." Basically: Nihilism is fun, but dangerous.

By the time Korine's next film, *The Beach Bum*, came out about seven years later, things had softened a bit. Again, it's a woozy and colorful tale of excess and hedonism. This time we follow Moon Dog (played by Matthew McConaughey), an epicurean, once iconic, Florida-based writer, across several wild nights of increasing intensity. He drinks, hoovers drugs, avoids real work or responsibility, has sex with anything that will let him, and escapes any consequences for his actions—including his own grief. Watching it, you feel like you've seen this movie before, you know to wait for the fall, when Moon Dog will collapse under the weight of his shirked responsibilities and the system will catch up to him. Except the fall never comes. During a brief court scene, even the judge is swayed by his charms and reputation.

After seeing the film at South by Southwest, film critic Hazem Fahmy wrote: "Rather than simply not address these issues, the film goes out of its way to remind us that nothing in this strange dimension truly matters." Moon Dog doesn't care about anything (or anyone); he lives for pleasure. Towards the end of the film he outlines his life's mantra to a reporter: "We're meant to have fun here."

For all this chaos, destruction, and clear disregard for rules, values, and consequences, Moon Dog isn't punished. In fact, by the end of the film he has casually been awarded a Pulitzer Prize and several million dollars. Although true to form, he ultimately shows they're meaningless too (I won't spoil the finale).

The Beach Bum is the most cheerfully nihilistic film I've ever seen. I liked it a lot. So did plenty of people I know. But many, many critics did not. At the time of writing, it had a Rotten Tomatoes score of 56 percent. The audience score was even lower at 30 percent. Multiple reviewers called it one of the worst films they'd ever seen. They were as disturbed by its grinning apathy as they were by *Spring Breakers'* glamorized violence. Sure, it wasn't a turn-of-the-century call to kill an aristocrat, but it was still a look at the chaos nihilism can welcome. Something that, years on, still terrifies many.

Nihilism reflects and feeds on our fears. But it also offers a warning about systems, the power they afford, and the values they champion. Nietzsche himself wasn't a huge fan of social norms and constructs. He believed they were gilded cages that limited our potential and gave us the illusion of meaning and something to lose. While he didn't identify as a nihilist himself, he still asked us to imagine a world where these systems were revealed to be an illusion that held no authority beyond what we agreed to place on them.

That's an interesting theory for millennials and Gen Z, who grew up within a reality where the structures that were supposed to provide our lives with meaning, a sense of larger purpose and stability, bind us together, and make us feel part of something were in such an open state of decay. Right now, institutions of government that once defined generational moral authority feel fetid and fragile. News institutions are under attack and are being reframed as an enemy, not a resource, of the people. Science is edged out by conspiracies and "wellness." Participation in organized religion is declining. And we're realizing that our conceptions of wealth and success are physically and mentally destroying us.

Political and moral nihilism warn us to not take any principle on faith, and to reject the idea that true and false, right and wrong, can ever exist absolutely. When Nietzsche argued that "Every belief, every considering something true, is necessarily false because there is simply no true world," he might have been speaking directly to our fractured "post-truth" reality.

Add to all that the knowledge that for many of us, the goals we were told to strive for (a house, a steady fair-paying job, the fantasy of retirement) are not only no longer available, but may have contributed to a capitalistic system of personalized greed and advancement that has crippled economies, bankrupted families, and strangled the planet.

In the Netflix sitcom *The Good Place*, the main characters spend a lot of time considering the meaning of life. During one episode the character Chidi—who conveniently happens to be a moral philosopher—has an existential crisis about the point of it all. During his breakdown, he walks a classroom of philosophy students down the major paths where humanity has previously attempted to locate meaning and understand how to live an "ethical life."

First he explains virtue ethics, where the likes of Aristotle champion central "virtues" such as honesty, courage, and compassion that individuals must strive for in order to live a meaningful life and contribute to a healthy society.

Then he moves on to consequentialism, which says you can judge whether an action is right or wrong by the resulting outcomes. In short, the right actions are the ones that make the world a better place.

Finally he explains deontology, which suggests society is ultimately directed and guided by a set of universal moral laws that we all agree to follow. It's apparent in everything from the Ten Commandments to the literal law.

At a glance, they're three pretty decent methods of assigning meaning and direction to life. Chidi goes on to declare all these theories wrong for reasons I won't get into because they're complicated storylines and you should just check out the show. But sticking with his framework of traditional ideas of meaning and purpose, it's easy to see why many young people could find their own fault with them. It's not that they're bad per se, but rather that they appear to be voided in practice.

Individuals in positions of power and authority are regularly absent of virtues. In fact, their ascent and success seem built on their lack of them. The right actions, say, like prioritizing an inhabitable planet over the interest of a handful of fossil fuel oligarchs, are rarely taken. At the same time, once-universal concepts like right and wrong, victim and criminal, protector and oppressor have become distorted debate subjects in an intensely partisan reality. With the basic tenets of goodness and purpose clearly scrambled, it's not surprising we've been called the Lost Generation.

WHY WOULDN'T YOU BE A NIHILIST?

So much writing about millennials and Gen Z is framed by their crushing debt, lack of steady employment, and the mental health crisis. Even if we wanted to buy into traditional myths of meaning and purpose, the pathways towards them—honest work, happy families, healthy bodies—are not always accessible. For those of us who came of age in the blurry decade bookended by 9/11 and the global financial crisis, the markers of a stable and meaningful life have become elusive.

In her devastating *Atlantic* article "Millennials Don't Stand a Chance," Annie Lowrey explains: "The Millennials entered the workforce during the worst downturn since the Great Depression. Saddled with debt, unable to accumulate wealth, and stuck in low-benefit, dead-end jobs, they never gained the financial security that their parents, grandparents, or even older siblings enjoyed. They are now entering their peak earning years in the midst of an economic cataclysm more severe than the Great Recession."

Speaking to *BuzzFeed News* during the depths of the 2020 COVID-19 crisis, twenty-one-year-old biomedical engineering student Hailey Modi looked forward: "Our whole lives, these structures have failed us and we are looking for political stances outside the mainstream— because we feel like we don't have time to solve these issues like income inequality and climate change. Incremental change isn't going to get us there in time to prevent [it]— this is dramatic, but it feels like a societal collapse."

Dissecting all the ways millennials and Gen Z came up short in the generational lottery has become something of a blood sport. My friends and I pick over articles coolly explaining why we're screwed with the grim satisfaction of peeling back a scab.

Few of these analyses are able to offer solutions or relief. The problems facing us feel too big, too rooted in history and choices made before we were even born. As Modi puts it, "We grew up in a world where things have already gone terribly wrong and our lives are just preparing for the worst." Honestly, after a few paragraphs of reading about all the different ways we're fucked, why we're depressed, and speculations on the new miseries that will carve up the next half century, I begin to disengage. I switch windows to Instagram or Twitter, turn on Netflix, put on my headphones, and submerge myself in the increasingly weird content that's being created within this vortex of hopelessness.

Here's the strange thing though: All that nihilistic content, the breezy jokes about death, the open declarations that existence is meaningless, kind of makes me feel better. Or at least it makes me laugh. "Generally, nihilism is regarded as a bad thing but there is, ironically, a bright side to it," writes Joseph Dillier in a column for *The Daily Illini*, the University of Illinois independent student newspaper. "We are waking up to our own misery. Our ironic nihilism is a product of our environment . . . Humor is our coping mechanism. What many people of the older generations take to be glib irreverence is just a way of processing an incomprehensible world."

As so many people can (and will) tell you, nihilism can take you to some pretty bleak places. Previous followers of it have been known to declare God dead, spiral into anarchy, and assassinate the odd government official. In *The Good Place*, at the end of his speech about how the traditional pathways to meaning lead nowhere, Chidi declares that nihilism is the only logical philosophical view. The realization causes him to have a total mental breakdown. Even in *Spring Breakers* and *The Beach Bum,* a more upbeat take on nihilism still leads to a lot of destruction. But credit where it's due, that's hardly representative of the more recent responses. In the real world, all those memes and calls for annihilation haven't resulted in hedonistic chaos. They appear to have had the opposite effect.

A NEW WAY OF THINKING

In the opening of a lengthy 2020 feature in *Paper*, the musician Kesha admitted, "I'm a nihilist, in that I think nothing matters." At first her statement feels worrying. In 2014 Kesha sued to void her contracts with her former producer Dr. Luke, who, as court documents explained, had allegedly "sexually, physically, verbally, and emotionally abused [Kesha] to the point where [she] nearly lost her life." The producer countersued and they entered into several years of legal gridlock where Kesha's experience of abuse not only became tabloid fodder, but she was also blocked from recording or releasing music that wasn't tied to her former label. Her choice was to work with her alleged abuser—or at least within a company that housed him—or to step away from music altogether. Viewed in light of that, it's fair to assume nihilism could be a destination for a despondent, trauma-frayed young woman. But she adds, "Then I think what really matters is just being kind. I have an existential crisis about once a day, on the low end." Nihilism isn't a pain point for her. It's a way to cope, stay centered, maintain perspective, and enjoy the moment. As she sings on the track "Tonight," off her 2020 album, *High Road* (which sees her embracing health and happiness after so much darkness), "We got it all if we're alive . . . If we're breathing, we're still breathing."

Later in the article she continues: "I obviously care about what other people do, especially politically, because it's affecting the entire world. But for me? I just want to write music that makes people feel good . . . I'm going to be as happy as possible because I could get hit by a bus in ten minutes. So fuck the world—in the most beautiful way." After spending time with her, author Jael Goldfine reflects: "When the past is painful, the future precarious, and you ended up getting sued for trying to change the world, 'Does it feel good?' becomes a prudent motto."

Like so many people posting bleak memes online, or tweeting at celebrities to hit them with their cars, Kesha found that nihilism could be an in-the-moment way to deal with personal loss, confusion, and fear. That sense of freedom, a release of control and expectations, is also present in the work and decisions of journalist and author Malcolm Gladwell—a man who has made a career researching why we act and feel the way we do. In an episode of his podcast *Revisionist History* Gladwell explores how nihilism applies to his life. Or rather, his hiring process. He begins by telling the story of meeting and quickly employing his first assistant, Stacey. Their "job interview" was brief, barely scraping beyond small talk; in less than an hour he had not only decided to hire her, but also hand over access to all his personal and financial information.

Usually tales like this are built around a warm spark, an incredible connection or instant feeling of "this person is the one." Gladwell didn't feel any of that. He just didn't want to interview anyone else.

Stacey's speedy hiring was undoubtedly partly driven by laziness. But it was also, he points out, an act of well-directed nihilism. Anyone who has ever dragged themselves through a job interview knows they're exhausting and repetitive dances of manners, buzzwords, rehearsed questions, and empty answers. No one is their true self in these spaces, and even if they were there's little way of really knowing if the person in the room would be good in the job. But still we carry on because we've been taught that this is the way things are done and assume that means it's the best option.

Malcolm Gladwell being, well, Malcolm Gladwell, is more cognizant of these familiar traps. He explains, "I look at all the folklore and ritual around predicting how well people will perform. And I say, 'give me a break.' I am an eye roller . . . I am a nihilist." He recognizes that "Life is a big crapshoot and most of the systems we put in place are there just to satisfy our illusion that we can see into the future."

Extracting himself from said "extravagant exercise in self-delusion," he chose to bow out of this grinding waltz and just hire Stacey. As things went, she was great and they worked together for years. He continued to make all his hiring decisions in a similar fashion. Occasionally things don't go well, but his nihilism continued to insulate all parties from additional discomfort. In an email to one less successful assistant he comforts them both with the sooth-ing reflection, "Some people are good at this kind of work, some people are not. It has no larger significance."

The liberation of boycotting meaningless decisions saved me a lot of angst while working on this book. While reviewing edits, the demand for my opinions quickly became more taxing than the writing itself. It also trig-gered my compulsion to overthink things. With each note I'd spiral: *What if this wasn't the right call? How would a reader I'll never know feel about this? Could this innocuous statement actually be deeply offensive? Had I unknowingly wandered into a topic I didn't realize was a flaming culture war trash can?*

Walking with a friend one afternoon I raved on and on about my insecurities. He listened generously and sympathetically, and offered: "It's understandable, this is kind of your opus." The statement, generous as it was, jarred me.

Was this my opus? Really? A seminal piece of work that would define and enshrine my heart and brain for future generations? I suddenly felt intensely embarrassed. All that nihilism hadn't prevented me from falling into this crevasse, but it could pull me out.

It was just a book, I was just a body, this was just a cold winter's walk. It was all so totally forgettable, pointless, impermanent. I knew this, but had again let myself partake in my own "extravagant exercise in self-delusion."

"This isn't my opus," I answered. He opened his mouth to loyally protest, but I stopped him. "This is meaningless, so why am I going on and on about it?" All those tiny decisions weren't building to some eternal, final achievement. They were just more time passing that I wouldn't get back. Time spent stressed and wracked with doubt.

I smiled at him, we kept walking, and the conversation turned to something considerably less painful. When I got home and opened my computer I returned to the field of edits. They were still time-consuming and complex, but they were no longer universe-altering events. They were just edits. They had "no larger significance."

PONDERING POINTLESSNESS

In 2020 the Northern Hemisphere's "summer blockbuster" movie season was interrupted by global shutdowns and stay-at-home orders, as countries struggled to contain the spread of COVID-19. Film releases were pushed back or moved to streaming platforms, and many wondered if the confused state of the world would impact what people would pay to see. Coincidentally, one of the films that broke out during this strange time just happened to touch on generational themes of pointlessness.

Looking back, it's not surprising that *Palm Springs* was a lauded hit during the early months of the pandemic. The film follows Sarah (Cristin Milioti) and Nyles (Andy Samberg), who are stuck in a *Groundhog Day*–style time loop that curses them to relive the same tasteful desert wedding again and again. At first, they do what people always do in these kinds of movies: freak out, explore inventive ways to kill themselves and others, gorge on booze and drugs, and generally destruct, only to wake up reformed the next day. They understand that everything they do is meaningless, a thought that is set to torture them for eternity.

The audience—stuck self-isolating at home for an unspecified period of time—found the frazzled yet charming pair unintentionally relatable as they pondered: *What's the point of any of this?* Watching Sarah and Nyles disintegrate, from my own stagnant reality I could sympathize. Stuck in a small apartment during a COVID-19 lockdown, each day the same as the one before, the passing of time only distinguished by the worsening news reports, I was asking similar questions.

Of course, Sarah and Nyles find a resolution, but it wasn't as simple as I'd expected going in. In the 1993 film *Groundhog Day* (the cinematic gem that cast the mold for the whole time loop genre), Bill Murray's character Phil escapes his hellish loop when he learns to be kind. It's a cozy, somewhat toothless message nestled inside a prickly film. Thankfully, *Palm Springs* goes in another direction.

While the filmmakers couldn't have known their project would be released during a period of global existential terror, they did know they were writing for an audience who had spent much of their life pondering pointlessness. As a result, I suspect they understood that a simple answer built around true love or self-awareness wouldn't cut it.

In *Palm Springs,* the time loop is eventually broken, but not before Nyles has a chance to understand that within the pointlessness of his literally nihilistic existence, there are still small moments of pleasure and beauty that give even such a meaningless existence value.

He, like Kesha and Gladwell, finds utility for his nihilism. It allows him to access an alternative point of view and a litany of delights that were previously invisible.

THE TRANSFORMATIVE POWER OF NIHILISM

As we've more than established, young people have a lot to be nihilistic about (whether they're stuck in a time loop or not). But gazing around, it becomes clear that those feelings are spurring more action than apathy. Nihilism has a way of forcing you out of yourself, and can transform our growing generational uncertainty and crisis of meaning from a tormentor into a motivator.

When we look at our lives and existence and ask, what's the point? we naturally frame the question from a personal perspective. But for a lost generation, so resigned to the idea that their lives will not be able to match their parents', that instinct has begun to shift. When you accept that you're hopeless, you're pressed to look for something else to save.

BuzzFeed News reporter Ryan Brooks's work has looked at the multiplicity of Gen Z's feelings of purposelessness. In the piece "Generation Freefall," he writes about students in New Hampshire who, aware that the compound mess of COVID-19 and a recession had sent their future plummeting, were considering abandoning their own aspirations: "Students told me they were so anxious about their futures and climate change that they were putting their education on pause to advocate for candidates and the Green New Deal." Their reasoning—that their uncertain lives may still be able to be pinned to a greater good—reflects the anxiety that also spurred Greta Thunberg to start the School Strike for Climate movement.

As a member of a generation confronted by catastrophic climate change—and the increasingly apparent health, economic, social, and political disasters that stem from that—Greta has also asked: "Why should any young person be made to study for a future when no one is doing enough to save that future?"

In the memoir *Our House Is on Fire: Scenes of a Family and a Planet in Crisis*—collectively authored by the Thunberg family—we witness an existential crisis play out from annihilation to action. Greta's first school strike, where she sat alone outside the Swedish Parliament each Friday, didn't come out of nowhere. It was a result of years of fraught domestic, mental, and personal reckoning that saw all the members of the Thunberg family cycle through periods of intense emotional distress. After a while, Greta's mother, Malena, began to question whether the problem lay with them or with the world at large. Maybe their anguish was a logical response to the climate emergency, and anyone managing to get up every day, eat a healthy breakfast, and not collapse under the weight of their own fear was the one truly acting irrationally. "We felt like shit. I felt like shit. Svante [Greta's father] felt like shit. The children felt like shit. The planet felt like shit. Even the dog felt like shit," remembered Malena.

So, entertaining this feeling, the family decided to do something about it. They turned their despair into a motivator and transferred the energy they had been pouring into the attempt to feel better as individuals into fighting the larger planetary problem. Reviewing the book in the *New Yorker*, Emily Witt wrote: "[Greta's] insistence on pessimism comes as a relief. The self-justification of any depressive person is that optimism is delusional, but the climate crisis presents a situation in which hope can emerge only from a collective acceptance of the dismal future."

Of course, this wasn't a one-off event. Greta has gone on to inspire millions of other young people who not only felt disillusioned by the response to the climate crisis themselves, but who also had lost grasp on the value of their lives in the face of it. They might not be able to save themselves, but once they'd accepted that, they could focus on saving the planet instead.

I thought a lot about where we put feelings of displacement and meaninglessness during the COVID-19 shutdowns, as so many of my friends lost their jobs and found themselves with few options for employment, stability, or even ways to fill their time. We were already locked out of so many pathways that had previously promised purpose, but now the road seemed even narrower. Each day, parts of our lives that had offered hope and pleasure were removed from us, until we began looking at each other and asking: What's the point?

One friend told me she couldn't bring herself to battle for a professional job anymore, choosing to embrace the unstable, part-time work she had begun stringing together to pay the rent. Not only was committing to the illusion of middle-class normality exhausting, but she admitted that it felt demoralizing to fuel a capitalist system that was so clearly failing. She opted to work as little as possible in order to survive and spend her time doing other things.

Work, money, success, the fantasy of the future contained no logical meaning for her anymore.

With so much open, unoccupied time, she and others began looking for ways to fill it. At first they baked, promised to upskill, learn a language, or get fit. Instagram became a variety show of fresh hobbies. But even these "hobbies," activities we were doing alone, away from each other, were tinged with an air of performance. There was a feeling that they still needed some meaning or reason for existing. As if a perfectly risen sourdough or short course on performance marketing might save us from a reality we had little control over.

Eventually, that all dropped away too, while the same questions returned: What was the point of any of it? What were we preparing for?

Then the footage of George Floyd's murder went viral, and the world was remade. Around the globe, life-long activists and first-time protesters took to the streets to demand not only justice for Floyd, but a commitment to restructure (or abolish) policing as we know it. As the movement got bigger and bigger, people from all communities found themselves examining their treatment of Black and indigenous communities, and how they related to people of color.

Where I live in Melbourne, the Australian city most impacted by the second wave of COVID-19, people didn't bake bread the second time around. They paid attention to how the virus and resulting lockdowns were falling on the population differently, in particular how residents of social housing were facing far harsher restrictions, over-policing, and considerably less government support.

The conversation went from "What's going to happen to me?" to "What's happening to them?" People stopped talking about their own job prospects or future, and began questioning the safety and dignity of the city as a whole. When reports from the residents most affected began emerging, detailing how many were isolated without access to food, toiletries, or medication, the city mobilized. Mutual aid groups popped up in those communities and were immediately flooded with offers of support. With so many people under- or unemployed, there was no shortage of offers to purchase, pack, and deliver supplies. Those turned away from in-person volunteer roles went online to sign petitions, create and share resource packs, call and email politicians, and drive fundraising efforts.

More than once (at home but also overseas) I noticed that when various protesters, volunteers, or newly minted activists were questioned about their commitment to community causes and disruption, they answered: "This is my job now." No one was going home or giving up until real change was actioned, traditional systems destroyed, and historic power fractured. There was, for the first time in a while, the feeling that maybe we could change something, create something new.

A nihilist understands that things will probably not get better for us as individuals anytime soon. They know the world is too broken to hope for a reasonable piece of it. But twenty-first-century sunny nihilists have shown the capacity this has to inspire action, not apathy. Because before you can be truly motivated to reimagine a new world, you have to totally lose faith in the old one.

THE MYTH OF
MEANINGFUL WORK

n the past, when people talked about meaning and the places humans have historically searched for it, they likely pictured churches, temples, libraries, salons, majestic mountaintops, and quiet corners that invite reflection and deep thought. Today, we have a tendency to seek it out in considerably more drab surroundings. In place of Epicurus's garden or Thoreau's cabin, we have office buildings, worksites, Zoom calls, and the many other poorly lit rooms where we spend our lives. As dour as it is to admit, our jobs have become home to some of our trickiest and most destructive entanglements with meaning.

Jobs, in theory, are simple things. You show up to a place, do a service that holds value, and are recognized for said valuable service with money, but also with the security that your job will exist tomorrow. That combination of fair pay and stability is supposed to elicit a sense of achievement, certainty, self-respect, and community spirit.

Growing up, I never asked my parents how they felt about their jobs, what they meant, or how they made them feel. I understood employment to be a boring necessity they endured because it allowed them to pursue things that made them happy on the weekend or after I went to bed. Whether a person was working across industry, service, management, content, agriculture, or information, a job was a job. Friends, family, nature, music, food, hobbies (and in my dad's case, books about historic naval battles) were a life.

When they had dinner parties, sometimes I'd catch an adult rolling their eyes about a boss or coworker, but work didn't invade personal time and attention far beyond that. Honestly, I could barely even tell you what my parents did for a living. Not that I didn't care. I could recall their interests, childhood friends, how they took their tea and coffee, but the intricacies of their jobs just seemed so removed from who they were as people.

Contrast that committed but apathetic obligation with the way so many of us think, feel, and talk about employment now. Doing the very impressive (or so I thought), very overwhelming job in digital media that I had from the age of twenty-four to thirty-one, I regularly worked twelve-hour days. But even when I wasn't at work, I was "at work." I thought and spoke about it constantly. All the major social and romantic relationships in my life were built around my job. It was by far the largest influence on how I spent my time, viewed the world, formed connections, and considered myself. Most nights I'd wake up, unprompted, at around 3 A.M. to read my emails. Sometimes I managed to resist the urge to pick up my phone, but even without its jarring blue light I rarely fell back asleep. Eventually a doctor told me I had so much adrenaline coursing through my body I wasn't able to remain unconscious for extended periods of time. My brain was literally trying to wake me up to get back to work.

When I held dinner parties, they had a noticeably different energy than my parents'. Every single one would devolve into a discussion about jobs, chronic stress, and how unhappy we all were. After a while I began to notice that this was a huge downer for the few guests who didn't share a dysfunctional relationship with employment. Rather than redirecting conversation, I simply stopped inviting those people over. It wasn't an act of malice—quite the opposite. I liked them too much to keep exposing them to this emotional pestilence.

You would think, considering how much of my life was dedicated to it, my job was very important or very well paying. It was neither. But still, my relationship to it was as complex and paralyzing as my parents' had been straightforward and fruitful. Their jobs were a tap running in the background that allowed them to grow a life, a family, and go on the occasional budget holiday. By my thirties, my job hadn't even offered the illusion of those things. But it did give me an erratic heartbeat that felt like there was a small bird trapped behind my ribs.

A lot has been written about how the workforce has changed since my parents entered it; the issues leading to the degradation of employment opportunities between then and now are massive and complex. I'm conscious of how we romanticize the seemingly smooth career paths of our forebears. The reality is things were already getting rocky when they were hosting their lower-key dinner parties. The fantasy of fair and dependable wealth has been fraying for the past fifty years as deregulation, globalization, swelling gig economies, and shrinking unions have eroded institutional worker protections.

My parents were affected by these shrinking markets, consolidated businesses, and deindustrialization. They faced regular unemployment and deep economic instability because of them. But their stress about work never seemed to be cut with the same existential dread as mine. If you were to ask them what they wanted, what it was all for, their answer would be clear: They just wanted to enjoy their lives.

Had you asked me the same question, in the middle of one of those email-checking nights, my heart and mind racing, I wouldn't even have known how to begin to reply. I understood that massive forces of capitalism had eroded what "a stable livelihood" could even look like for me. That the original equation of employment—you show up to a place, do a service that holds value, and are recognized for said valuable service with money and security—was largely voided. So what could be offered in its place that would demand my full attention, loyalty and commitment, and come to consume so much of my life? Easy: meaning.

I should pause for a second to differentiate between meaning and value at work. All jobs have value, some obviously so: healthcare professionals, frontline workers, plumbers, human rights lawyers, teachers, etc. But even the most mundane play a part and should be respected. When I was a retail assistant or a waitress, I helped others find snatches of pleasure in their day. Editing a digital publication, I worked on content that made people laugh and think. While writing this book I worked part-time for an ethical dog food company; it made me feel good to know we were helping people take care of their pets. All these jobs paid me, and I in turn spent that money, propping up an economy that allowed others to be paid and the hometown that I love to grow and change day after day. The problem is at some point we began to feel like "value" wasn't valuable enough.

In her *BuzzFeed News* article "How Millennials Became the Burnout Generation" (which, on publication, became an instant classic in the bloodshot eyes of everyone I know), Anne Helen Petersen broke out the expectations millennials now hold for their jobs. While they still hope for "employment that reflects well on their parents (steady, decently paying, recognizable as a 'good job')," they also dream of work that's "impressive to their peers (at a 'cool' company) and fulfills what they've been told has been the end goal of all of this childhood optimization: doing work that you're passionate about."

Boomers throw their necks out shaking their heads at the idea young people need to feel special at work. But that feeling of specialness is sometimes all work can offer us. It's tempting to make fun of the wide-eyed desire to have a job that matters, that inspires passion and maybe also cultivates a little envy. But is it really so wild for a group of people who understand that the historic rewards for hard work are becoming increasingly elusive to hope to emerge with something?

It's simplistic to imagine that before the global financial crisis, everyone who graduated from high school walked straight into a thirty-year job and a secure mortgage. But the path to a "good life" was undeniably clearer. Most of the people I know have accepted that many of the trappings of an idyllic middle-class existence are not available to us. We don't dream of our parents' backyards, leisure time, or retirement funds. But with those historic rewards removed we need something to sustain us, especially as the work itself becomes more competitive and demanding. Waking up in the middle of the night to read emails is unbearably grim if you know you're doing it to achieve a whisper of advantage over your equally overburdened, under-slept coworkers in the eyes of a boss who will probably never notice (or care about) your sacrifices. But telling yourself that you're doing this because the work matters, is meaningful, and makes you abstractly more valuable renders the surging pressure less crushing for a moment.

In my own life I began to observe how the fantasy that my job had meaning allowed me to fetishize my overwork and exhaustion. The long hours, poor pay, and monumental ability to, as I called it, "eat shit" morphed from a depressing reality into a point of pride. My capacity to exist within a demoralizing job, economy, and employment landscape started to appear as a marker of my strength, focus, and specialness. In turn, the performance of work and stress became its own reward and currency, a way to signal my value to others. If I was this stressed out, I must have been doing something truly important.

This strange muddle of "meaningful work," busyness, and performance seeped into all areas of my life. Time itself became a commodifiable resource that always needed to be committed to the pursuit of something—self-betterment, enlightenment, financial gain, efficiency, optimization—in order to in turn also be christened "meaningful." Within a mindset where stress and busyness demarcated value, empty minutes were wasted and I was only as good as I was productive.

Jenny Odell explored this phenomenon in her book *How to Do Nothing: Resisting the Attention Economy*, reflecting that "in a world where our value is determined by our productivity, many of us find our every last minute captured, optimized, or appropriated as a financial resource by the technologies we use daily." It was a trap I happily fell into, becoming a loyal disciple of what Odell calls "capitalist productivity."

Even now, I schedule most of my waking hours to block out time not only for meetings and appointments, but also for seemingly spontaneous events like "read the news" or "say something nice to someone." I compulsively use apps that track and quantify how I move my body, as well as what I buy, eat, and look at online. To make sure I'm not missing anything, I've recently begun wearing a smart watch that provides insights on my heart rate, step count, time spent standing, and what's hazily referred to as "movement," which I've come to understand as calories burned. It's terrifying, but also strangely thrilling to know so much about myself. To submit the mysteries of my body and mind to numerical evaluation and have them presented back to me as graphs and goals. It's seductive to witness meaning and purpose, once so elusive and confusing, be transformed and delivered by a buzzing accessory that tells me to stand or drink a glass of water. Life's biggest obsessions—how to be happy, healthy, a responsible tenant of my own body—are wrangled down to earth by a push notification.

I'm honestly not sure what I'm trying to achieve when I break my Sundays into thirty-minute increments, or adorn myself with tech that threatens my personal privacy in pursuit of invasive data, but the sense of control and power this way of living offers is comforting. Approaching my sparse leisure time with the same steely commitment I apply to work makes me feel like I'm using my life *right* by not wasting a moment. Even when I'm grinding through mundane tasks like folding the laundry I'm able to trick my brain into thinking the effort is meaningful simply because it is being so intensely commodified and tracked.

This somewhat dystopian desire to transform ourselves into perfect, optimized, always-on workers has the dual effect of also making us perfect consumers (that smart watch cost $300, by the way). Even now that I've left my stressful job, I still struggle to sleep through the night—something my watch reminds me of often, but does little to actually help with. A lack of sleep is a side effect of all this endless optimization. It's also a business opportunity.

MEANING AS A PRODUCT

Not surprisingly, I often wake up tired, and find my usual morning coffee can't help me out. So I walk down to a local café and buy a second coffee that contains some combination of mushrooms, roots, and bark that promises "to support mental stamina, alertness, and concentration." It also costs eight dollars. At lunch, if I'm still feeling out of it, I pop a green effervescent tablet (fourteen dollars for a tube of ten) into a glass of water. The fizzing elixir apparently has "eight real greens and only ten calories to support healthy aging, better circulation, and antioxidants for glowing skin." Of course, I could just cook and eat a bowl of greens, but that would take time, which I can't spare, especially on a workday. A while ago, I found myself on the *Goop* website (they have a lot of content about sleep), examining a packet of preselected and portioned vitamins called Why Am I So Effing Tired? This mix of ninety-dollar nutrients is "designed to help support balance in an over-taxed system." Ninety dollars is equal to several hours of work for me. Several hours of emails that I'll no doubt read in the middle of the night, frying my brain, driving me back to the eight-dollar dirt-flavored coffee. Standing in line to order it, my mind sometimes drifts back to that ice cream that wasn't allowed to "just be an ice cream." I understand I'm falling for a trap I once helped set, but still, I really need this embarrassingly expensive coffee to be more than just a coffee. I need it to mean something, to signal that my day, and ultimately my life, will get at least eight dollars better.

No one understands this weird dance better than Arianna Huffington, the founder and longtime editor in chief of media startup the *Huffington Post*. During the past decade she's turned her focus to a second empire built on millennials' inability to get some rest. In 2010 her TED Talk "How to Succeed? Get More Sleep" went viral. Six years later she followed it up with her book *The Sleep Revolution* and announced that she was leaving the *Huffington Post*. She wanted to focus on her health startup Thrive Global, which is specifically interested in addressing stress and burnout.

It's an admirable ambition, although somewhat tainted by allegations of toxic work culture, underpaying (or simply not paying) contributors, and arguably being an architect of a style of aggregate churn-and-burn journalism that destroys young writers and erodes trust in the news media at large. But credit where it's due, show me a better example of "capitalist productivity" than building a media brand on the backs of underpaid, overworked young content creators, toiling away at a "meaningful" job they believe will "make a difference" until they crack, at which point you sell them the dream of finally falling asleep.

I get it. I look for meaning to make this all seem worth it, but become trapped in a system of consumption that requires me to spend my hard-earned cash on expensive crutches to make me feel human in a world that treats me like a machine. That thought depresses me, so I remind myself that my work is meaningful and start the cycle all over again, a little more tired, a little more broke.

Not only do I participate in this strange loop of work, destruction, and consumption by buying into the myth of my own stress and the value it apparently signals, I actively project it. Even on quiet days, when asked how I am, I instinctively answer "crazy busy." As if "stressed" has replaced my former baseline of "fine."

THE EXPLOITATION OF MEANING (AND YOU)

The tricks we play on ourselves are at times depressing, but always understandable. The myth of meaning is seductive. It infuses the boring or stressful parts of our lives with a sense of purpose and offers a way to soften the tougher realities of our working existence. When the size of your paycheck or the pleasure of your job isn't enough to get you out of bed, the dream that it's meaningful might be. But it's dangerous when these fantasies—and how they can propel us to endless work—are weaponized by employers. Meaning, for as much weight we give it, is a desperately cheap offering: easily proposed and advertised. Because of this, it's an invaluable currency in many workplaces.

We've probably all seen (or experienced) this: An employee (likely very young) is recognized as valuable, so how do you nurture and motivate such people without simply paying them more? You allow them to gorge on the fantasy of their own importance, the meaning of their work, their influence, their own cultural power. Help them loom so large in their own minds, lives, and careers they don't have space to glance around and ask: Do I actually want this? Is this even good for me?

I was working on this chapter when Apple launched their much discussed and criticized "working from home" advertisement. It follows a small team trying to balance the stress of living and working through a pandemic with increased family pressure, a sociopathic boss, and a mounting pile of impossible demands. Rather than standing up to their employer, and questioning a system where they're asked to work harder and harder with diminishing time and budgets, the group knuckles down. Led by a fully indoctrinated and hypermanic team leader, they find new and inventive ways to make the impossible happen, never pausing to question the logic of this madness or expecting to be thanked or rewarded in any way.

They work while they eat, brush their teeth, look after their families, exercise, tidy their houses, and ignore their kids. This pace is kept up through the night, robbing them of sleep and rest. The ad's big conclusion is, I think, they finish on time? It's supposed to be funny, watching a group of human beings decimate their lives to get the job done. In actuality it's deeply depressing, especially when you realize that by the end we're supposed to see them as winners who have achieved something meaningful—with the help of several Apple products.

I recognized myself in the ad. I've fallen into this trap more times than I'd like to admit, so desperate to believe I was something special that I never paused to wonder why, or acknowledge that deep down I knew myself to be acceptably, but undeniably, ordinary. It felt good to slip into the narrative that I was somehow destined for great things. Fueled by the sense I was someone, with something meaningful to offer, on the precipice of some opaque greatness, I'd stoically soldier on. Working endlessly for stagnant pay, even as more solid dreams (home ownership, a family, a car that was younger than me) slipped past.

BECOMING THE PROBLEM

When talking about the exploitation of our desire for meaningful work, it's easy to cast the villain as some older, Machiavellian type, whispering toxic affirmations in the ears of soft-brained millennials desperate for their student debt to have a purpose. But buying into meaning doesn't always mean you become the prey; it also holds the trickster charm of turning you into the predator.

To look around today, the most creative and successful peddlers of meaning at work aren't boomer bosses leaning over unergonomic desks telling you your menial labor is making the world a better place. They're Glossier shined, Everlane wearing, Veja footed, here to announce that your daily grind isn't just a job, it's an act of resistance, rebellion, protest, and self-care.

When faced with the fallacy of work as religion/identity/community, you have a few options: be consumed by it, reject it and reckon with the existential void that opens up (more on that later), or join in.

Browsing bookshops or online today you might notice that the self-help and personal development section is evolving. Yes, there are still the usual texts about yoga, meditation, positive thinking, and (hopefully) nihilism. But increasingly, work—the thing we're supposed to come to this sage-scented genre to escape from—has invaded.

These books have titles like *Get Rich, Lucky Bitch!*; *The Audacity to Be Queen*; and *Nice Girls Don't Get the Corner Office*. I have no doubt that many of them offer thoughtful advice about navigating the aforementioned traps of exploitative work culture. But they all hover around this same idea: Work, handled and treated right, can make you happy. The thing is, to get there you need to give it your all—live it, breathe it, meld it seamlessly with your entire life.

The past few years have been crowded with examples of this kind of work-as-life, get-it-done, and get-yours thinking. Again and again it promises enlightenment, identity, purpose, community, and connection through an eighty-hour workweek. But too often what's delivered is far more disturbing.

Perhaps most infamous among this flock of authors is Sophia Amoruso, the much discussed and debated founder of Nasty Gal and Girlboss Media. Amoruso's career began when Nasty Gal was just an eBay store selling (often shoplifted) vintage clothes. In her book #GIRLBOSS, she explains that she shoplifted because her political ethos at the time "didn't really jibe with working for the Man." The store was a hit, and soon enough Nasty Gal had become one of the world's fastest-growing companies. By 2016 Forbes named Amoruso one of the richest self-made women in the world. She'd actually left Nasty Gal by then, and the brand went on to file for bankruptcy. In 2015 the company was sued for allegedly firing women just before they were about to go on maternity leave.

Elsewhere in #GIRLBOSS Amoruso reflects: "I entered adulthood believing that capitalism was a scam, but I've instead found that it's a kind of alchemy." The second kind of alchemy in play was meaning. Combined together they can transform our desires to consume, make money, and draw attention to ourselves into something more appealing—in this case (and many others), empowerment.

While much has been made of Amoruso's tale, she isn't the only one to use meaning to reconfigure a desire to be successful and presumably wealthy (which is fair enough in itself) into an outwardly social, community-driven, meaningful act. The promise of empowerment through commerce has created a swelling stream of feminist-approved capitalism.

Similarly styled and aesthetically pleasing companies like Thinx, Away, Outdoor Voices, and the Wing have since slipped in behind Nasty Gal and Girlboss Media to actively blur the lines between identity, product, feminism, ideology, and employment. They've also gone on to puncture said fantasy through varying reports of staff mistreatment, crushing performance expectation, bullying, gaslighting, underpaying, and providing inadequate maternity and HR support.

To be clear, this is by no means a market exclusively cornered by women. Perhaps the most infamous, bombastic, confusing, and ultimately catastrophic example of meaningless meaning at work can be attributed to Adam Neumann, the pseudo-tech-bro-messiah who became very famous and very rich with his coworking startup WeWork. For anyone insulated from this tale of a millennial Icarus, WeWork is a company that provides flexible shared workspaces to freelancers and small businesses. Launched in 2010, it's a service that makes a lot of sense as traditional office setups become less rigid.

Neumann didn't invent the coworking model, but he did a transformative job of selling it to the public, staff, clients, and investors. His vision wasn't just a way to enjoy the convenience of an office without the management headaches. He presented it as a revolutionary new way to work, where access to free beer and meditation pods would rewire brains, productivity, and literally (although always opaquely) save the world. WeWork wasn't a slightly atypical real estate business but a "meaningful" utopian community where members could redesign society as we know it—and, you know, have seltzer on tap.

All this magical thinking hit its limits when the company was nearly destroyed by a disastrous IPO and cascading internal accounts of hedonistic (and deeply cringy) excess, hubris, mismanagement, and truly nightmarish-sounding staff parties.

In a scramble to save a version of the business, thousands of employees were let go and Neumann departed. Although not before engineering an exit package worth hundreds of millions of dollars.

You can get lost in all these horror stories and articles. There is a feeling of schadenfreude in seeing ambitious people fail (especially when you're not harboring such lofty ambition yourself). But you can hardly blame anyone for getting caught up in all of this (I'm surely not immune). A nice aspect of this version of seeking meaning through work is that it might actually (emphasis on "might") make you rich. But it has another bonus: It allows us to view the world as we would like it to be. Offering a life where success and personal advancement can somehow still serve a higher, noble purpose. It's what Facebook's chief operating officer Sheryl Sandberg preached with her book and online community, *Lean In*. In Leigh Stein's *Medium* article "The End of the Girlboss Is Here," she reflects on the unique sleight of hand that seeks to imbue work with meaning. Looking at Sandberg's book in particular, she unpacks this curious combination of "woke capitalism" and social justice: "*Lean In* offered a game plan for success in the corporate workplace through the lens of self-improvement. Sandberg never set out to dismantle the system, but to excel inside it . . . By presenting gender disparities in the workplace as a war to be fought on a personal level, Sandberg allowed women to feel like they were activists whenever they advocated for themselves."

This compulsion of Sandberg, Amoruso, and so many others is understandable and appealing. When we talk about finding meaning in work, naturally we are exploring it from a singular, personal perspective. What will this job promise, achieve, or deliver to me? The myth of meaning at work offers a wonky loophole that lets you chase money, success, and power while still maintaining the warm, fuzzy feeling of rejecting the capitalist systems that have knee-capped entire generations. Basically, yes, you can have nice things and keep sharing activist epitaphs on your Instagram feed.

But someone always eventually pays. Even when we (and by *we* I mean a very slim few) manage to navigate the "meaningful work" quagmire expertly enough to not be personally exploited, someone still will be. This system of buying into meaning and purpose, of allowing yourself to be taken advantage of (or to take advantage of others), works because it preys on that extra-tender part of ourselves that longs to be recognized as special. After all, isn't that what meaning is ultimately suggesting? That you are on a unique path, destined for something extraordinary? Notions of specialness are supposed to make you feel good, but gorge on them and they'll also make you an asshole.

Working all the time, barely sleeping, and treating your body like a fragile exotic plant renders the most mundane parts of our lives impossible: We don't have time to cook, shop, clean, socialize, or decide what to watch on TV. The only way to get these basic tasks done is to partake in new economies of convenience that have been designed for our burned-out brains, to give us illusions of the real lives we're missing while working so hard for some magical future existence.

You can't waste your precious, valuable time on an evening unwinding with a glass of wine and a slow-cooked risotto, so here's a delivery box full of pre-cut, plastic-packaged, long distance–shipped vegetables. With no time to shop, let Amazon make it so effortless to buy things that you forget you've somehow given up the ability to spend fifteen minutes mindlessly browsing a store. To our parents, this kind of assistance would have required exorbitantly expensive services like chefs, assistants, personal shoppers, and drivers. No matter what generation you're part of, that's not affordable for the masses. So for us to keep using them, to allow ourselves to keep working, these services must become very cheap.

Corners are cut. The delivery driver goes without insurance, the warehouse worker without breaks (or, more recently, personal protective equipment), the rideshare operator without maternity leave. Viewed with perspective, we know this is wrong. So how can we accept it? We do so by believing that we are special, that our work is meaningful, important, and must be completed by any means necessary (just like those poor saps in the Apple ad). We're conditioned not to think about the life of the driver picking us up for an 8 A.M. meeting, because the meaning we've tacked onto our work inflates us to such giant proportions within our own minds we can't see anyone else.

We believe work makes us valuable and gives us purpose, so we welcome it into our homes as if it were keeping us solid. Who are you without a constant flow of emails, or a constant flow of complaints about emails? To be stressed is to remind ourselves we exist, we matter, someone wants something from us, even if it's more than we can give.

Our jobs are consuming because they matter, they matter because they consume us, and to step away, and suggest any other, more nihilistic reality would be to cast our whole professional existence as a farce. It's heartbreaking to consider that we've been tricked into wasting so much of our lives. So we keep going, burrowing deeper, looking for something that makes it all feel worthwhile. Because now, to stop seems like the craziest act of all.

A REAL CRISIS REFRAMES A FAKE ONE

That was, until COVID-19. It feels glib to suggest that it took a disease that at the time of writing has infected almost 200 million people, killed over four million, and brought global economies to a grinding halt to make us question the meaning of our endless work. But it did.

With the virus sending whole cities into lockdown, crippling much of the travel, hospitality, and retail industries, supercharging unemployment rates, and trapping millions of people at home, many of us became stranded in a strange new half-life where time was no longer demarcated by achievements or disappointments. Social media posts about workouts, side hustles, and pulling all-nighters were replaced by photos of knitting projects and softening bodies. For those of us who weren't performing frontline jobs, responsible for the terrifying life- (and country-) saving work of keeping our cities open and our bodies safe, the world became both much larger and much smaller overnight.

Our existences, which previously spanned workplaces, suburbs, and physical interactions with other people's bodies, were shrunk to the square footage of our homes. While our minds—which had so recently felt full up with thoughts of ourselves and our own work—expanded exponentially to try to digest a once-in-a-generation event.

One of the strangest things to me was how at first we tried to apply our ideas of work, meaning, and potential to lockdown. We carried our momentum—of having to perform, be productive, complete tasks—blindly into the most stressful period of our lives and thought it would help. At first everyone promised to use the extra time productively, pledging to exit lockdown with a book, a finished PhD, the ability to run a 5k. We tagged each other in exercise challenges, made complex and photogenic coffees, and plundered hardware stores for DIY projects. These habits were so ingrained that even at what was casually called "the end of the world" we performed as capitalist worker bees.

But soon, that too came undone, as the narrative we'd ingested about being hyper-optimized machines finally failed. The meaning we coveted and looped through our jobs, that allowed others to exploit us and us to exploit others, started to feel empty and cheap. Our emotions, fear, and exhaustion weighed us down. We hit the limits of optimization and began to remember we were tender humans after all.

I'll be honest with you. Writing this chapter made me feel insane. Sitting at my desk, cataloguing how I became the kind of human who obliterates their body with work, patches it back together with self-care, believes my specialness makes my behavior elevated, and logs all my psychotic acts on an expensive watch that tracks and reports my every move, is beyond dystopian. I get that.

But for so long, the alternative seemed even more terrifying. A few years ago, when I was in my early twenties, and first dipping into a simmering, stressful work culture that would eventually boil, my boyfriend suggested that I quit my job. He saw it was making me unhappy, and wondered what was the point? I was appalled and offended at the thought. I couldn't believe that he would think for a moment that my job—which, to be clear, was entry-level media, mostly copy editing, admin, and writing the odd newsletter—wasn't a vital act.

I was happy to accept the praise of people who assured me that while they could only give me menial tasks and minimum wage, I was clearly a very special and rare commodity.

The truth, which I was almost a decade away from admitting to myself, was that I had nothing else going on in my life beyond that job. It was easy to slip into the illusion that it was important and special because I was so desperate to feel that something about me was. In reality my job didn't matter, and neither did I.

I remembered this recently when reading a piece by an ex-coworker. In his *VICE* article "Maybe Your Big Dream Is Making You Unhappy," the very talented Julian Morgans reflected on the feeling he got watching documentaries that grappled with the endless expanse and chaos of space. Admitting that he found them hard to watch because: "They remind me how we're just on a little rock in space and how everything we value is tiny and insignificant, and the only antidote I can think of to all that cosmic irrelevance is an illustrious career. It sounds ridiculous, but the emptiness of space makes me want to leave my mark. Not for its own sake, but because irrelevance is frightening. Being noticed here on Earth feels a bit like carving my name into a large tree. It's a way to signify: I was here, briefly."

I relate to the feeling that a job might bind you to existence, but the sunny nihilist in me respectfully disagrees. Seeing a job in the context of the universe doesn't have to be demoralizing. It can be freeing.

For most of us, work is an unavoidable necessity. But the destruction that can come from overinvesting in it isn't. I enjoy my jobs (like many writers, I juggle a few), and most days I don't feel the hours I spend on them are wasted. But sometimes I do still find myself unmoored by a busy schedule, challenging meeting, or tough feedback. That pressure follows me home, burrowing into my brain, pushing me to question what the whole arrangement says about me, my choices, the way I've constructed my life. I worry about what it means. In the past, that could start a grisly descent into panic and pain. But now, I do like Malcolm Gladwell and remember that no matter how the day went, my work "has no larger significance." It can provide value (to myself and others), but not meaning.

This trick brings me back to myself, breaks me out of my toxic mythmaking. I accept the reality that nothing I ever do will allow me to definitively say, "I was here." My work, even if it was brilliant, will eventually be forgotten in time. And even if it's not, I won't be there to enjoy the attention anyway. My fixation on it won't save me. But it could ruin my day—or someone else's. That future, the one we're all working for, is just an illusion, pulling us away from the present we're already so lucky to enjoy.

These days I ask myself different questions about work. Instead of, *What does it mean?* I try, *Am I well? Do I have what I need? How about those I love?* In contrast to people's former impressions of nihilism, my divorce from meaning moves thoughts from attention and reward to community and family, health, and safety. My energy doesn't pool around myself, but redistributes to the spaces I once found impossible to make time for. I call my mom, donate what money I can spare, go for untracked runs, and feel happy not because I am special but because I am not. I'm just a body moving through space. I consider the moment I'm in. I know I have no control over it, so I don't count it, assign it value, or promise it to something larger. It will pass quickly and never return. I enjoy it the best I can and let it go.

We were told that our work was meaningful, that our jobs would make us better, save us, make us whole. But when sunny nihilism pulls focus from them, we see a new reality take form. One with lower stakes, pleasures at hand, simpler answers, and achievable goals. Meaning will never be attained, because it doesn't exist. But respect, care, delight, space, a phone call with a loved one, an action to help another person are available right now. They don't offer a mystical reward, one that will involve you giving over your body or mind, buying into a devil's bargain. They only ask that you stop obsessing over what might be, and allow time to experience the euphoria of what already is.

FOLLOWING YOUR HEART
(INTO THE VOID)

first became aware of the human race's collective and totally consuming fixation on romantic love through music. While being driven home from primary school, the radio stuck on classic FM, I'd listen to men and women across decades and genres lament and celebrate it. They crooned about "Endless Love," "The Power of Love," the "Greatest Love of All," promised "I Will Always Love You," because they "Can't Help Falling in Love," presumably because "Love Is the Drug." Song after song, day after day, year after year, it was the same story. To my congealing preteen brain it seemed a bit excessive.

Sure, a few tracks made sense. In many ways, romantic love is the first system of meaning we're taught. Before we've grasped the brittle concepts of theology, morality, and worth, we know love. We desire, offer, obsess over, and are happily consumed by it. At nine years old or so, I wasn't immune to early stirrings of love. I understood it bound my parents, inspired Disney movies, and would eventually demarcate my own entry into the land of grown-ups. Already doomed with the tendency to crush on anything with a pulse if it paid me a fraction of attention, I didn't consider myself above love's charms. But even my narrow life, bound by how far I could ride my bike without getting in trouble, contained other equally confusing and torrid emotions. Days were full (and I mean full) of jealousy, regret, joy, fear, anger, elation, wistfulness, nostalgia, hope, and boredom. I wasn't even allowed to write with a pen yet and I was flooded with feelings. Surely these people on the radio, who were privy to all the mysteries of the adult world, had a few other things to talk about?

Eventually I asked my mom why people only seemed interested in writing love songs. After a pause she answered, "People have a lot of feelings about love. It's the most important thing in the world."

"Important" is a pretty subjective term. But you can't deny love's influence. For centuries it has monopolized our attention through art, media, and consumer habits. But unlike other systems of meaning, such as work or religion, we're slow to criticize love or even admit that our obsession with it is making us miserable.

You can hardly blame songwriters (or my mom) for getting swept up in the cosmic grandeur and comforting fantasy of love. The idea that we're spiritually defined and even physically formed by it is ancient. The Greek philosopher Empedocles in the fifth century BCE suggested that the world was made of four primordial root elements—air, earth, fire, and water—that were drawn and fused together by love. Plato took the idea of love's guiding effect on our lives, bodies, and souls even further. In the *Symposium* he presented the Myth of Aristophanes: a foundational parable of predestined love.

The story goes that in the beginning, humans were round like planets with four arms, four legs, and two faces on opposite sides of their heads. There were three genders: one made up of two male bodies that was descended from the sun, one made up of two female bodies that was descended from the earth, and one made up of a female and a male body that was descended from the moon. This unorthodox design was a big success. People were happy, fulfilled, and powerful. They could run backwards and forwards, as well as cartwheel and tumble in elegant circles—which apparently was a big deal. Things were going so well for these fleshy, multi-limbed orbs that the gods began to see them as a threat, and worried they would attempt to challenge them and claim their own portion of celestial domain. Zeus, the king of gods and men, decided to stop any future coups by slicing the humans in two "like a sorb-apple which is halved for pickling."

The separation, understandably, was physically and emotionally agonizing. These perfectly contented and aligned pairs found themselves alone for the first time. From then on, they were cursed to search for their other half in the hopes of reforming and returning to their previous state. Only when reunited with their missing other would they again experience true love and companionship. Their trauma can be seen as the germ of our own obsession with finding a "soulmate." To exist without this mythical other half is to remain severed, wounded, and incomplete. Since then, love has held steady as one of our favorite places to search for meaning and fulfillment. Although over the centuries our expectations for what that means have grown exponentially.

Meaning and purpose are complex and movable ideas. But one constant is that they exist as foils to make our daily existence more bearable. To believe that life—and our place within it—has a larger point is to wish for all the pain and suffering we experience daily to ultimately be *for* something. But love stands apart from other systems of meaning in what it promises. It doesn't attempt to wrangle the narrative to make the ugliness of life feel a little easier or more worthwhile. Love promises to transform life itself.

THE LOVE MAKEOVER

Each new love is a fresh start, a chance to remake ourselves, to be seen and known as we wish to be. Once, during the sweetest rush of a new relationship, I bounded into work with all the sizzle of someone freshly in love. At the time I was a retail assistant at a boring and repetitive job that I was widely recognized as being terrible at. Hours staring at beautiful people and beautiful clothes usually left me feeling worn out and ugly, but on that day, something was different. I made easy conversation with customers, the concrete floors didn't seize my lower back, and the harsh overhead lighting couldn't wash out my flushed cheeks. Glancing at myself in an eternally unflattering full-length mirror, I didn't see the usual sight—all dark circles, blotchy skin, and greasy hair. I saw myself through the eyes of the person who loved me. Witnessing me skip past, a coworker observed, "Oh, you have your love mojo." She was right. I felt great, like a hyper-capable, charismatic, more valuable version of myself.

This kind of transformation had been available to me before. Prayer, meditation, work, and therapy all gesture at pathways to self-acceptance and betterment. But they also require a lot of effort. In comparison, falling in love is easy. In a few weeks, someone's lusty, adoring gaze had given me a feeling of satisfaction that would (eventually) take years of therapy to reach alone. It felt like a shortcut to knowing myself. When asking the eternal question, *Who am I?*, is there a more appealing answer than *I am loved*?

To be loved is to exist, to matter, to have a purpose—even if that purpose is to be an object of someone else's desire. That's not love's only trick of course. Just as love mutates our sense of self, it also alters our wider perception of reality, spilling over to make everything feel special.

Who hasn't walked down the street, brimming with love, so sure the air has never been crisper, the sun brighter, or passersby more beautiful? Louisa May Alcott observed in *Little Women*, "Love is a great beautifier." It shows how malleable meaning can be by making everything feel meaningful.

Even lost or unrequited love manages to pull off a version of all this. Laura Ashe, Associate Professor of English at Oxford's Worcester College, reflects in the *Oxford Arts Blog* on our enduring appreciation for a sad love story: "In a tragic story, sorrow is made into a meaningful pattern, even into something beautiful. If you allow that pain can be profound in literature, it creates a space for your own emotions to seem meaningful rather than chaotic." What other system of meaning offers such a golden parachute? Even when it fails, love doesn't leave us empty-handed. A broken heart is still a token: a symbol that you hold a capacity to love, and a reminder that love may eventually return, once again igniting existence with purpose and splendor.

THE (COMPLICATED) EVOLUTION OF LOVE

When you're in it, love feels like a totally unique and personal experience. You wonder how any other creature could have ever felt like this. How human bodies around the world continue to think, walk, and eat while trying to calibrate such a heady rush of emotions.

But writing these words, remembering my own experiences and those of friends, writers, and musicians, a familiar patchwork appears. For as individual as it feels, we engage with romantic love as if it were a quantifiable emotional monolith that everyone experiences the same way.

We're not able to speak about love in this shared language because it is an inherently fixed, knowable thing, a permanent object we can pick up and pass around, but because we have created and perpetuated a version of it that is. Like all systems of meaning, romantic love as we experience it is invented and learned. As seventeenth-century French author and memoirist François de La Rochefoucauld famously noted: "There are some people who would never have fallen in love, if they had not heard there was such a thing."

In his article "A Cultural Perspective on Romantic Love," Dr. Victor Karandashev writes: "Love emotions are experienced by many people, in various historical periods, and in most cultures of the world. Yet, these feelings display diversity—cultures influence how people feel, think, and behave being in romantic love." Tracing back through history, it's not tricky to spot how shifting attitudes around romantic love speak to social expectations about how individuals are expected to live and behave.

Prior to the Middle Ages, in the West, romantic love was considered more of a liability than a blessing: an irrational cocktail of emotions that could lead you astray and threaten rather than strengthen the institution of marriage.

Unions between people were business and family matters, a way to secure and expand wealth, reputations, and security. They needed to be considered, negotiated, and entered into with clear minds—not overflowing hearts. Love would perhaps be tolerated in the young, but was expected to be shed like baby teeth before the onset of adulthood.

This sentiment is visible through generations of literature and art. Ancient Greek myths are full of loving tales that result in murder, betrayal, abandonment, and bad decisions, with couples regularly being turned into animals, plants, stones, and even the odd river. Romantic icons like Ovid's Pyramus and Thisbe and Shakespeare's Romeo and Juliet are treasured by sentimentalists now, but were originally offered as warnings of how the irrationality of romantic love (and failure to listen to your parents) could literally be deadly.

The rise of twelfth-century French court poets, known as troubadours, softened romantic love's reputation a little. These artists dedicated much of their work to the topic of love, but even they didn't suggest it was something to build a life (let alone an identity) around. For troubadours love was a passing fixation, something to fawn over for fun. They dedicated their works to women they never intended to sleep with or engage in any real sense. Not uncommonly they never even met their muses, but rather were guided and inspired by reports of their beauty. Love was a distraction, a way to pass time or inspire art while not diverting too much attention from more serious matters. It could exist because it wasn't automatically placed under the burden of existing within a marriage, or alongside life's less engaging but more pressing matters.

Marriage provided stability, structure, legacy, and purpose; love offered fun and pleasure. As a result, they were often kept separate—embodied by a spouse and a lover. It wasn't only accepted that people (well, men) might exercise these more frivolous impulses outside of marriage, it was often seen as the more responsible action, one that allowed the primary relationship to stay steady by not letting matters of the heart rock the business of marriage. Love was like a glittering bauble, something to admire and be entertained by, but not to be assigned any real meaning.

Things began to change with the rise of the artistic and intellectual movement known as Romanticism in late eighteenth-century Europe. Converts to Romanticism didn't believe passionate, romantic love was a passing folly, but a vital, life-giving force that should be expected to exist uninterrupted for the life of a relationship. Whereas before it was largely understood that an individual's emotional needs might be met through several relationships (wife, lover, friends, God), Romantics returned to Plato's original model, and argued that they should all be fulfilled by a single, perfect partner who would instinctively know and understand everything about them. For them, love should be instant, complete, perfect, meaningful, and eternal.

Romanticism, like all systems, served a role beyond being, well, romantic. It was a response to the Enlightenment, the industrialization of England and

Western Europe, the rise of science, and the retreat of spirituality in public and private life. This transition was fueled by the dawn of the industrial age. As (mostly young) people streamed into urban centers, they picked up freshly created jobs in newly built factories and emerging industries. These expanding chances for employment brought independent sources of income, and in turn allowed some the freedom for the first time to make their own choices about how to live. Away from the control of families, choosing a partner could be influenced by new ideas and values related to love.

Love as the basis of a marriage and a life was a new concept, embraced by the young and derided by the old. It said, *Don't worry about what your family thinks, follow your heart*. As traditional avenues of meaning frayed, love offered an alternative, a new sense of cosmic purpose. But for a revolutionary practice lit up by the idea of trashing existing expectations and pissing off your family, the Romantics' version of love introduced as many boundaries as it dissolved. Rather than abolishing ideas of marriage or presumptions between partners, it remade them to be impossibly whimsical.

In the hands of Romantics, love became increasingly complicated. Previously, a good marriage was one that was secure, to someone who hopefully treated you with a basic level of respect and care. Now, a good marriage was an eternal state of bliss where emotions never faltered, sex never disappointed, and both parties were rewarded with a feeling of destiny being fulfilled.

What Romanticism started, marketing eventually perfected. The nineteenth century saw the rise of commercially produced Valentine's Day cards, published guides on how to write love letters, and a boom in women's magazines marketed to the middle classes that gave detailed advice on finding and keeping a husband. The Romantics' new version of love might have been radical, but its participants were still hungry for rules and conventions that stated that they were doing it *right*. Advertisers in the twentieth century recognized this desire for new traditions that felt old, validated relationships, and (conveniently) created sales opportunities. Slogans such as "A Diamond Is Forever" became entangled with our own oral histories of how to love and be loved, as conventions with a long list of easy-to-follow steps led people from dating to wedded bliss. Marketing departments popularized these rituals, each with associated purchases: a box of chocolates on the first date, engagement rings, bridal showers, bachelor parties, wedding dresses, honeymoons, anniversary gifts of paper or tin, recommitment ceremonies, and even divorce parties. Don Draper, the infamous ad executive from the TV show *Mad Men*, wasn't overestimating his influence when he quipped: "What you call love was invented by guys like me to sell nylons."

Modern romantic love evolved into a finely tuned performance to be studied and replicated. To reject these productions, not play into the grooves they set, puts you at risk of being excluded from the experience altogether, cursing you to remain unpicked, alone. In her 2012 book

Minimizing Marriage: Marriage, Morality, and the Law, Rice University professor of philosophy Elizabeth Brake introduced the term *amatonormativity*, which she explains as "the assumptions that a central, exclusive, amorous relationship is normal for humans, in that it is a universally shared goal, and that such a relationship is normative." Romantics promised that love can offer meaning by making us feel seen, known, understood, and transformed. But by the twentieth century the commodification of love also offered the assurance of normality. To be loved was to be chosen, classed as correct. To be without love was to be defective, incomplete, sliced in half by Zeus.

All systems of meaning offer a perceived reward in exchange for compliance. We allow ourselves to be controlled and directed in the hope that it will lead to a sense of purpose and acceptance. Love is no different: behave in a way that is lovable, learn the language, buy the trinkets, treat love with the deference it deserves, and enjoy an eternity of unblighted bliss, total recognition, spiritual clarity, and bottomless meaning. With a prize as attractive as that, it's easy to lose sight of what's being asked of you in return.

We assume love is good for us because we've been told so many times that it's the case. But spare a little thought for what it literally and figuratively costs. Unfortunately, for all the big talk of the Romantics, and of the ad men who followed, the data doesn't paint such a rosy picture of modern romantic love unlocking a feeling of completeness.

Paul Dolan, a professor of behavioral science at the London School of Economics, explored just how blissful eternal love actually is in his book *Happy Ever After: Escaping the Myth of the Perfect Life*. Looking at the happiness levels of married, single, divorced, separated, and widowed individuals, he found that these "happily ever after" arrangements did, to be fair, serve *men* pretty well. Speaking at the Hay Festival in 2019, Dolan addressed married men by saying: "You take less risks, you earn more money at work, and you live a little longer." The outcomes were not so sunny for women. Rather than finding fulfillment in long-term romantic relationships, married women were generally less happy and tended to die sooner than their single sisters. "The healthiest and happiest population subgroup are women who never married or had children," he added.

A (BRIEF) DEFENSE OF LOVE

Romantic love is easy to poke fun at, and this isn't to say that any entanglement with love is a fool's game. Once you get past the misty visions of soulmates and bodies with two faces, there are some pretty strong arguments for falling in love—they're just not as poetic as we might like. Plato and Empedocles imagined love as an elemental force that existed absolutely, as real and knowable as gravity. That expectation is often placed on systems of meaning. We like to think of them as fundamental, rather than functional. But while the way we express, appraise, and think about love is learned, the essential feeling itself is not. The instinct to love is embedded in our bodies and brains. It informs and influences what it means to be human. Like jobs, it has value, even if it doesn't have meaning.

Biological anthropologist Helen Fisher has long been interested in what happens in our brains when we fall in love. In 2005, she and her research team published the results of a study that looked at MRI scans of college students' brains when they gazed at an image of someone they were deeply in love with. They compared the results with a baseline of brain activity when those same students looked at an image of an acquaintance. After reviewing 2,500 scans they observed that looking at photos of lovers resulted in more activity in the regions of the brain that makes dopamine. Explaining her findings to *WIRED* in 2017, Fisher said: "This factory is part of the brain's reward system, the brain network that generates wanting, seeking, craving, energy, focus, and motivation." The brains of these people in love were producing a natural high that was comparable to amphetamine-style drugs.

Alongside dopamine, when we're near someone we love our brains release oxytocin—a neurotransmitter colloquially known as the "love molecule." Oxytocin makes you feel good and intensifies a sense of connection between people. It also lowers anxiety by reducing the stress response of the amygdala, the part of your brain that clocks danger and responds by releasing hormones that get you ready to fight, flee, or just feel extremely tense. Paul Zak, a professor of economic sciences, psychology, and management at Claremont Graduate University in

California, has looked at oxytocin's impacts and found that it can lower blood pressure and heart rates—especially in women. It also tends to spike when romantic partners hug each other for twenty seconds. Which explains why when we're anxious or afraid, our partner can often make us feel more soothed than anything else.

In his *Atlantic* article "Love Is Medicine for Fear," Arthur C. Brooks looked back to the observations of Chinese philosopher Lao Tzu, who two thousand years ago wrote in the *Tao Te Ching*, "Through love, one has no fear." Brooks observed that a couple of millennia later, the suggestion that "love neutralizes fear" was literally confirmed by science.

Beyond comforting us at moments of high stress, love also acts as an emotional lubricant to help ensure we carry out some of the physical necessities of life. In his key 1819 work *The World as Will and Representation,* German philosopher Arthur Schopenhauer identifies a central force that he believed drives all humans: the will to live. He argues that the will to live is more vital than any other learned compass of morality, ethics, or reason, as it's what motivates humans to go forward, survive, and continue. It's not a sophisticated desire for meaning or purpose, but rather a simple need to exist for another day, as part of a species that will hopefully exist for another millennium. In short, it's about sex. In Schopenhauer's eyes, the only arguable "meaning" to life is the creation of more life.

Let's pause for a second to acknowledge the crushing heteronormativity of that attitude, and how it excludes people who can't have or don't want kids. Obviously there is more to life than humans with reproductive capabilities using them. But that fixation does explain in part why humans (who choose to have children) benefit from love.

If you are in love with someone you may be more likely to have sex with them. Although, no disrespect to Schopenhauer, history has a lot of evidence of people happily having sex without love. In a heterosexual, contraception-free pairing, that sex may lead to a child. Viewing childbirth without the romantic narratives we've spun around families and togetherness, it's hard to see it as anything less than an objectively terrifying, dangerous, chaotic event. Pair it with ideas of love and connection, and it starts to feel a bit more doable.

Love (hopefully) connects you with your partner and increases the likelihood you will be able to work together to keep this new being safe. Even if you're not in a position to conceive yourself, love may drive you to take in another child and ensure they play their part as a healthy link in a biological chain, keeping Schopenhauer's will to live ticking along for another generation.

While marriage is historically an uneven union that puts an extra onus on women and makes many people miserable, there's no doubt that the survival of our species is reinforced by the creation of social groups. Feelings of love help us cooperate, compromise, reason, and sacrifice. Cohabitation is an innately stressful state. But giving up things you like, making allowances for another person, and accepting sacrifices to ensure they're safe and well are easier to do when you love them. Without it, few of us would be able to be so selfless and caring, day in and day out, for the amorphous goal of "the good of the species."

In thinking about love, you often find yourself in a catch-22: We need love to thrive and survive, but our obsession has blown up to the point where the expectations we place on it are making us miserable (especially if you're a woman). All systems of meaning carry impossible demands, but love has the unfortunate addition of usually heaping all these onto (usually) one person. I love David Bowie, but when he sings "Everything I've done, I've done for you" on "Within You," I squirm. It also irks me when Jerry Maguire declares "you complete me" or David Copperfield claims that his beloved Dora is "more than human." Rather than swooning, I just think: *God, that all sounds like a lot of pressure.* No one can live up to our own standards when it comes to love. We expect it to transform us, give our lives meaning, and grant us eternal bliss. Any failure to be perfect feels like a defeat.

TAKING THE PRESSURE OFF LOVE

Within that whirlwind of purpose it's easy to lose sight of the basic pleasures of love itself. While we're focused on eternal meaning we forget about momentary happiness. Viewing love as preordained, fundamental, and inevitable takes focus off the joy, luck, and privilege of it. When I look at my partner, I don't tell myself that the universe conspired to bring us together, I focus on the chaos embedded in our relationship. It's wild to me that we met at all. That we were both born within a few years of each other, ended up in the same city, in the same social circle, and happened to meet at a point in our lives when we had the emotional capacity to commit to another person.

In the grand scheme of the universe, our love is pointless. It may impact the movement of our lives, but I know it will change little else. It is not fated, or written in the stars. It is a tumble of chance. When he makes me happy, I marvel at the brain that floods me with feelings and the body that lets me express them. When I find myself frustrated by the grind of respectfully cohabiting with another person, or when we have a twenty-minute conversation about the correct way to pack a dishwasher, I take a breath and review my expectations for what a relationship should look and feel like. I ask myself: *Who designed and laid out the stories and standards of love that I have consumed up until this point?* Thinking back over all the books, movies, and songs that don't mention dishwashers, I remember that they are fantasies. But by buying into them, believing they speak to some core tenet of existence, I'm doing nothing but causing myself pain, not to mention saddling the person I care about most in the world with expectations no flesh and blood human could ever meet.

To self-soothe, I remind myself that love will not save me, transform me, or give me meaning. It's just one of countless meaningless acts I will participate in over my lifetime. But luckily, it is one that has the capacity to occasionally bring me real joy. I know that the feelings of happiness my body produces when my partner is near are physiologically real; other preoccupations—my desire for love tokens, total understanding, and endless bliss—are inventions. Some created by me (notions of what I want my life to be), some created by others (visions of what a "correct" life is). By separating the two concepts I can feel the former more fully and dismiss the latter.

This nihilistic approach to love at first seems chilly. But nihilism—and the acceptance that the love we feel is a survival tool we've come to sentimentalize—strips the experience of loving someone of pretense and expecta-tions. Sometimes after sex I lie there thinking about what just happened. I understand that the passing pleasure is a trick my body has learned to make me happy, bond me to a mate, and perhaps one day produce offspring. Love is a gift—delivered by my brain through dopamine and oxytocin—that I can use, define, and enjoy. That's enough for me. I try not to ask anything more from it. My life and my ideas about love are my own to shape.

Philosopher and social theorist Simone de Beauvoir understood this. She didn't see love as something that happened to her, rendering her passive, but as a concept she could control. She assigned it her own practical (but still aspirational) expectations. In *The Second Sex*, her 1949 exploration of the treatment of women through his-tory, she argues for "authentic love," which prioritizes freedom over complete soulful fulfillment. De Beauvoir took issue with the existing socially created myths of love and the values they placed on individuals. She chose to see authentic love as being reciprocal and equal, declaring that it needed to benefit all parties, who should support each other while on their own personal, eternal paths of "becoming." She didn't suggest love completes you or makes you whole, but that it carries you while you find these answers yourself and express your own agency. Love was an ingredient or resource to be called on, given, received, and repurposed as needed, not worshipped as a finite state or idea.

De Beauvoir doesn't diminish the importance of love, but she also doesn't allow herself to be controlled by a prescribed version of it.

By rejecting (or reinventing) the idea that we can find meaning within romantic love, we're free to appreciate it fully, to be charmed and strengthened, but never crushed under its weight. It becomes a passing joy, one to appreciate and be thankful for, but not mourned for when it fails to meet invented standards or disappears completely.

Countless writers, philosophers, scientists, and artists have tried to dissect love and the role it plays in our lives and communities. But even the most clinical minds would struggle to deny it altogether. As humans we're built to love, have sex, and enjoy ourselves. But our minds too often wrest these joys from our bodies, and assign them impossible expectations. Love will never solve all our problems or give life meaning, and to expect such things ultimately spoils it completely. Our dreams of perfect love curdle the pleasure, comfort, and strength it can offer. Love is best enjoyed as an addition and a pleasure to behold, but not something to stake your whole life on. What a miraculous piece of luck it is to experience, even if just for a second. It's a meaningless gift, not a final answer.

LIFE AFTER GOD

wrote this book in Melbourne, the city where I grew up and have lived since childhood. In the months it took me to complete, the world was devastated by COVID-19, and my beloved but usually pretty low-key hometown transformed into the epicenter of the Australian outbreak. Responding to the crisis, the state government introduced some of the tightest restrictions in the world. I drafted this chapter at the midway point of a 112-day, stage four lockdown. Residents were only allowed outside our homes to exercise once a day, buy groceries, or access essential services—all of which had to be done masked and alone. Needless to say, it was a stressful time.

Speaking to friends and family, over Zoom or through headphones on a daily walk, we debated and theorized what was going to happen next. Between swapping vaccine theories and lamenting high school friends turned conspiracy theorists, there was an echo: "How will it all end?"

It's easy to forget how, at the beginning of the pandemic, things felt briefly surmountable. When the numbers were low—and for those of us living on an island at the edge of the world, the crisis, far away—people liked to talk about what this unparalleled break from normality "meant." We told ourselves it was nature hitting back after centuries of abuse, a call from the universe to slow down, some cosmic reminder to get to know our neighbors better, or finally tidy up the balcony. Clearing out cupboards, archiving family documents, and calling old friends, so many marveled, "I never would have gotten to this without a pandemic." We looked for reason within the blooming chaos, because reason and meaning are the superstructure we've been taught to build our lives within.

But as COVID-19 progressed, we ran out of hobbies and began to miss our busy lives. The articles optimistically positioning the crisis as a space for personal growth and reflection dried up. We edged back from the narrative that maybe this all had a point, and gritted our teeth (behind masks) to get through it.

That was for everyone except my mum, who has remained stoic, optimistic, thoughtful, reflective, and resilient throughout. She never appears to have a really bad day or lose a grip on her emotions. I've been calling her a lot, and finding her unchanged by world-changing events is comforting. While she also talks about enjoying the chance to clean out her garage, she holds another advantage that long ago slipped by me: She believes this terrible, stressful time is part of God's plan, and has faith we can locate reason within our pain. In the middle of a once-in-a-century disaster, she finds shelter in one of humanity's most primal spaces to seek comfort and purpose: religion.

Despite growing up in the church, I no longer consider myself religious. But sometimes I feel like there's a cavity in my brain, formed by Sunday school, emptied by time, and now left vacant for any number of undefined systems of meaning and purpose. And I'm not alone—many nonbelievers carry a feeling that we're missing something. We do so because in many ways, humans evolved to trust in forces larger than ourselves.

Charles Darwin believed that religion was a defining part of being human. In *The Descent of Man,* he observed that a belief in God was "the most complete of all the distinctions between man and the lower animals," adding that "a belief in all-pervading spiritual agencies seems to be universal; and apparently follows from a considerable advance in man's reason, and from a still greater advance in his faculties of imagination, curiosity, and wonder." While there are countless variations of what we mean when we use words like "God," "afterlife," "prayer," or "religion," a century of anthropologists has backed Darwin in the opinion that almost every culture on earth developed alongside some belief in a higher power.

But while its presence is universal, the specific role of religion is still debated and unclear. Scientists, anthropologists, philosophers, and psychologists are divided over why we consistently seek out or invent gods. Speaking to the *New York Times* in 2007, psychologist Jesse Bering, author of *The God Instinct: The Psychology of Souls, Destiny and the Meaning of Life,* suggests that belief is instinctive: "We have a basic psychological capacity that allows anyone to reason about unexpected natural events, to see deeper meaning where there is none . . . It's natural; it's how our minds work." Evolutionary biologist Richard Dawkins is a little tougher on this natural state. He calls our urge to place meaning in the hands of a higher power an evolutionary accident, and posits: "Religious behavior may be a misfiring, an unfortunate byproduct of an underlying psychological propensity which in other circumstances is, or once was, useful."

THE UNDERSTANDABLE APPEAL OF BELIEF

Misfiring or not, our brains want us to believe in *something*. There's a literal pleasure in faith—as anyone who has ever been "taken by the spirit" can tell you. For a period in my childhood, my family attended a Pentecostal church whose services involved calling people forward to be prayed over. Those sessions were often an orgiastic performance of screaming and crying where usually prim church members thrashed around, wailing at the heavens and calling out to

Jesus before dropping to the floor, sweaty and exhausted. People regularly needed to be carried to their seats, being so overtaken by the experience they couldn't walk.

As a kid, down for any kind of show, I'd sometimes take part myself. While I never had one of the aforementioned breakdowns, I did feel *something* course through me.

Later at home, behind closed doors, with all the secrecy of a séance, my friends and I tried to recreate the experience. Pushing palms into each other's foreheads, attempting to ramble in tongues, we were desperate for another kick. It never worked when we were alone, but we kept trying. Years later, sneaking drinks and joints in those same bedrooms, I wondered whether my childhood desire for prayer and my teen interest in getting high were connected.

According to researchers at the University of Utah, I might have been on to something. Led by neuroradiologist Jeffrey Anderson, they've studied that sweeping feeling, found in what they call "reward-based neural systems." In their work, they observed the brains of young Mormons (using MRI machines) who were "feeling the spirit." Reporting on their efforts for *WIRED* in 2016, journalist Liat Clark explains: "The participants were asked to press a button whenever they were experiencing heightened spiritual feelings. Time and again, the reward circuit regions of the brain were activated at the same time as the participants pressed the buttons most frequently. These are the same sections of the brain that instigate dopamine release during drug-taking, enabling addiction."

Andrew Newberg, a neuroscientist and author who has also looked at how religious experiences impact us physically, lays out the brain's response to a higher power in his book *How God Changes Your Brain*. He writes: "If you contemplate God long enough, something surprising happens in the brain. Neural functioning begins to change. Different circuits become activated, while others become deactivated. New dendrites are formed, new synaptic connections are made, and the brain becomes more sensitive to subtle realms of experience. Perceptions alter, beliefs begin to change, and if God has meaning for you, then God becomes neurologically real."

His work led him to suggest that religion serves two functions for our brains: self-maintenance and self-transcendence. It helps us cope, process information, and understand our surroundings by assisting us in defining a sense of self, personal values, and identity. For thousands of years, religion offered a prism through which to observe our world and ourselves. It explained forces and occurrences for centuries before science elucidated them. But while our brains might still crave a higher power, the world, starting with the Age of Enlightenment, has been actively challenging the broader role of religion.

Leading thinkers, philosophers, and historians of the time (like France's Voltaire, Germany's Immanuel Kant, and England's John Locke) challenged people to consider that knowledge could be gained through experience and learning, rather than from religion as a primary source. They argued that the mysteries of the universe weren't questions of spirit, but tangible problems to be wrestled with, unlocked, and understood.

Ultimately, the Enlightenment gave us a lot—modern concepts of liberty, freedom, governmental responsibility, and the French and American revolutions, just to start. But the best efforts of Voltaire, Kant, and Locke couldn't totally disrupt the will to believe in something beyond ourselves. Two hundred years later, it's clear that religion's command over us is due to more than knowledge gaps or brain chemistry.

Participating in acts of faith inside huge buildings of stone and concrete, reading from hulking books that have been lauded for millennia, it's easy for us to feel religion is fixed and finite. But what we choose to believe says a lot about what we need and want during specific points in time. In the ancient world, gods tended to be chaotic, cruel, and selfish. Their behavior was a way to explain patterns of life that were terrifying and unfair. With the growth of monotheism, religions such as Judaism, Christianity, and Islam moved ideas of God away from pain and fear to focus more on care, morality, and wisdom. God became a way through trauma, not a cause of it.

LOSING OUR RELIGION

Seeing religion as a house for meaning and purpose, it's understandable why it became a pet subject (or target) for nihilists. Nietzsche himself is perhaps most famous for declaring "God is dead" and that "we killed him" through our elevation of science and reason. Ironically, Nietzsche felt our will to believe was deeply nihilistic. He argued that religion didn't enrich life, but soothed by offering an escape from it. Viewed like this, one could argue that the suggestion we toil on Earth in exchange for an afterlife or other future redemption dismisses the value of life as it exists right now. Therefore, by rejecting God, we can face the present, looking at life without preconceived notions of meaning or morality.

I suspect that Nietzsche would be happy to see the current state of religion. Gallup reports that in 2020 "47% of Americans said they belonged to a church, synagogue, or mosque, down from 50% in 2018 and 70% in 1999." Presently, the Public Religion Research Institute states that 25 percent of Americans claim they have no formal religious identity. Ironically, that makes them the single largest "religious group" in the United States.

As my own experience reflects, the shift away from religion is largely being led by young people, with the Pew Research Center stating that four in ten millennials claim not to be affiliated with any faith.

It's difficult to speak broadly about why people turn away from faith, or choose not to engage in the first place. Even examining my own drift from the church, there is no splinter point where I was aware of thinking differently. Over time a tether just seemed to fray. That initial euphoria subsided and rooms that once felt like they housed God just felt like ordinary rooms.

But holding all this data against my own experiences, general patterns do emerge. Religion may have provided meaning and guided morality for centuries, but it's clear that for a new generation, former answers are falling short. Less than half of millennials feel that a belief in God is a prerequisite for a moral life. In fact, the statistical analysis site *FiveThirtyEight* has reported that "a majority (57 percent) of millennials agree that religious people are generally less tolerant of others, compared to only 37 percent of Baby Boomers."

But just because we're not finding the answers to questions around purpose and goodness in God doesn't mean we've given up on the topics altogether. Arguably, no generation has ever had as many avenues for the exploration of meaning. Just as we're freer than ever to define our own identity, sexuality, gender, and family, we're less invested in binary belief systems. The internet has ensured that we're no longer tied to the ideas of people in our immediate company, so we're able to move between existing religious structures, as well as browsing concepts of self, community, and virtue through alternative spiritual traditions, activism, wellness, politics, and even secular "cults" like fan culture.

So far, this exodus doesn't seem to have hindered our ability to be good people. Studies have shown that kids raised without religion can be more tolerant towards others and more resistant to peer pressure. Although being able to generate our own sense of right and wrong hasn't stopped us investing in the fantasy of meaning.

Nietzsche hoped the decay of traditional religions would push us to question why we needed them at all. He wanted people to stare into the abyss of meaning and imagine themselves without gods. But it's here that his hopes for a post-religious existence begin to crumble. Because while the data suggests a decline in religious participation, it isn't truly fading away, but undergoing yet another transformation. Rather than morph into faithless Richard Dawkins clones, many of us have invited fresh fixations to take its place.

LOOKING FOR GOD, FINDING COMMERCE

For all the criticisms we can heap on religion, you can't deny that for a long time the system has worked for a lot of people. As established, my mom is one of them. One afternoon, chatting with her, I laid out some of my feelings on why meaning was overvalued and over-trafficked. Every time I offered an argument, she would return to the same answer: "The meaning of life is to serve God."

You'd think I, a sunny nihilist, would be frustrated by her response. But I left that chat more envious than irritated. There's a part of me that's jealous of the clarity and simplicity religion can lend to life. I'm glad someone I love so deeply was gifted the ability to believe so fully.

Religion provides a framework for us to interrogate meaning and looming questions of existence. It also offers a sense of connection (be it to God or to a community of worshippers), guidance, and room for transformation and absolution.

In the biblical book of Second Corinthians, Paul writes: "We all, with unveiled face, beholding the glory of the Lord, are being transformed into the same image from one degree of glory to another." It's such a nice idea. That through God our sins can be forgiven, our souls wiped clean, and we can become better, purer versions of ourselves. So nice in fact, that long after I gave up my nightly prayers I continue to chase that fantasy through habits and rituals that speak to my lingering desire to be watched over and transformed. I cross my fingers for luck, wish on birthday candles, avoid cracks in the pavement, and beg anyone who will listen to protect me during bumpy flights. Even those of us who can walk away from meaning remain entangled with the dream of direction and metamorphosis.

When I was a kid I briefly wanted to be a nun; I liked the sets of rules and divine objectives. I pictured living as a medieval saint, walled away, dedicated to work, with a direct line to God and a snaking queue of pilgrims waiting to see and be impressed by me. It spoke to my desire for goodness, government, and attention. That's a weird childhood aspiration to remember now. But glancing around my apartment, bathroom, makeup cabinet, reading list, and the screenshots on my phone, I don't think I'm alone in wanting those things. In the past decade, they've been reflected in the ever-expanding wellness (and more broadly self-help) market, which similarly promises to align minds, bodies, and souls through an endless scroll of advice on how to reach a state of purity and peace.

At the time of writing this, the wellness industry is worth well over four trillion dollars. Since 2015 it's expanded at a rate of 6.4 percent annually—double the speed of global economic growth in general. Its huge rise is complex—tied to our disconnection from traditional health services and twisting expectations of how our bodies are supposed to age, look, and work. But I'd argue it's also a response to that cosmic vacuum so many of us have in our brains after leaving religion behind.

In place of priests and rabbis we welcome influencers and celebrities, who also offer to wipe our souls and bodies clean. Scrolling through Instagram, passing beautiful people elegantly exercising, stretching, clutching crystals, and anointing themselves with homemade tinctures and green smoothies, the patterns of devotion are familiar. Where I used to take communion to be absolved on a Sunday, I now Google twelve-hour cleanses and attempt a salt bath.

The blurred lines between religion and this opaque but very recognizable mash-up of undefined "spirituality" aren't a total accident. Many of these dewy-skinned, photogenic, blandly palatable influencers learned their best moves at church. If you spend a lot of time online, saving and pinning visually appealing images of colorful drinks, peppy quotes, and elegant living rooms, chances are you've come across the Christian influencer scene—even if you didn't realize it.

Figures like Rachel Hollis, Meredith Foster, Carlin Stewart, and Marissa and Bec Karagiorgos silkily slip between self-help, wellness, fashion, lifestyle, and Bible talk, showing how interchangeable they can be. Scrolling through accounts like theirs, it's easy to confuse Bible passages with generically #blessed platitudes as they instruct followers to be fearless, reject toxic thoughts, practice gratitude, and drink smoothies. Once the affirmations have been rendered in the looping cursive or pastel colors of Instagram, it can be hard to tell where they come from. Although it doesn't seem to matter too much in the long run, they all get to the same point: Follow us to become a better version of yourself.

Of course, you don't have to stick so close to the literal outlines of religion to seek out meaning in the twenty-first century. Other fixations provide a comparable framework with an even more opaque sense of spirituality. Speaking to *Market Watch*, Melissa Jayne, owner of Brooklyn-based "metaphysical boutique" Catland, reflected on why our current generation is so drawn to alternative systems of meaning: "Whether it be spell-casting, tarot, astrology, meditation and trance, or herbalism, these traditions offer tangible ways for people to enact change in their lives . . . For a generation that grew up in a world of big industry, environmental destruction, large and oppressive governments, and toxic social structures, all of which seem too big to change, this can be incredibly attractive."

Astrology in particular may be the primary cultural force challenging wellness as a generational obsession.

The history of astrology is ancient, stretching back thousands of years to Babylon and spanning the globe; versions of it are practiced from China to Greece. During its lifetime, astrology has shown a tenacious ability to adapt to our needs and impulses. But the current, most visible iterations have been largely stripped of early context, and repurposed for a religion-free, meaning-hungry audience.

Astrology today lives and thrives as part of mainstream culture. Asking someone their sun, moon, and rising signs feels as natural as inquiring where they grew up. Even if we don't "believe" in the personality profiles and daily predictions, countless numbers of us still partake in the rituals. Religion is about transformation, but it's also about understanding ourselves and others. Astrology presents a similar service. We know (or some of us do) that the scattered stars above us, and the times and dates of our birth probably don't assign our lives innate, immovable purpose. But they do give us a shared language with which to negotiate values and desires.

New York magazine's resident astrologer Claire Comstock-Gay has written about astrology's staying power, saying that "while advancing scientific knowledge offered other, more verifiable ways of understanding weather or crop seasons or politics, our private inner worlds, and our messy, complicated relationships with each other remained wild and mysterious, never fully explainable by science."

When I think of astrology in the present decade, my mind goes to Co-Star, the AI-powered astrology app that since launching in 2017 has been downloaded over three million times and collected over 1.6 million Instagram followers. Its success is predicated on an understanding of what a new generation needs and values: vehicles for meaning that are as convenient as they are enlightened. Cofounder Banu Guler has said: "There is a belief vacuum: we go from work to a bar to dinner and a date, with no semblance of meaning. Astrology is a way out of it, a way of putting yourself in the context of thousands of years of history and the universe." Religion used to take a lifetime to locate meaning, but in the twenty-first century its delegates have streamlined the process to make it almost surgical.

As Co-Star, consumer-aligned wellness, and religious influencers can attest, meaning is an innately marketable product. So it's not surprising that brands have caught onto the message that our desire for meaning, guidance, and redemption makes us a broad target market. As established, to be a successful, beloved millennial or Gen Z brand, you can't only have a good business model. You need to also *stand for* something. Increasingly companies have leaned into the role of high-minded authority, to reflect the themes of community, transformation, and identity that define religions. Perhaps the most visible recent dealer of this strange mash-up of commerce and spirituality is video-streaming exercise bike phenomenon Peloton. During a pandemic that canceled communal workout sessions and made the outdoors risky, Peloton evolved from a popular, occasionally controversial exercise provider to a full-on cultural phenomenon. Although the success of Peloton can't be attributed to extraordinary circumstances alone.

Despite having a business model that requires people to spend thousands of dollars to avoid leaving their home, Peloton is big on "community." Users are encouraged to join live classes where they can chat, cheer each other on, and exchange virtual high fives. Instructors attract huge followings (in class and on social media), serving as niche celebrities of sorts. Popular classes—with their pumping music, charismatic, headset mic–wearing leaders, and devoted disciples—are said to have the feeling of a mega-church extravaganza. Except rather than being surrounded by a crowd of worshippers, you're at home, alone, sweating it out on the spot. Users get Peloton tattoos, attend conventions, meet friends and life partners "on the bike," and are often quoted as calling the program, and its leaders, "life changing."

To be clear, while I find the Peloton frenzy fascinating, I'm not surprised (or judgmental) about it. For years I was a disciple of a very photogenic Pilates studio where young people who looked like me would strap ourselves onto tortuous reformers and repeat small, agonizing exercises. I started to go because I wanted to look better than expected in my swimsuit. I kept going because the soft-voiced, gentle instructors interspersed their calls to tuck in my pelvis with open-ended, existential questions about our perceptions of self, ambition, happiness, and physical vanity. After a few months I noticed that at the end of an especially hard day I'd scramble to nab the last spot in an evening class, hoping the instructor might say something illuminating enough to untangle my brain and give me a passing moment of peace. Maybe, if I were a few decades older, I would have turned to a house of worship on the way home. Without it, I made do with my blondewood studio.

Our eagerness to seek out and commit to new proxies of faith is understandable. After all, historically, religion has given countless people comfort and guidance, a sense there is something more to life, and the comforting assurance that we and our actions have a purpose. Research has shown that adults who have a connection to spirituality are generally happier than those who don't. They're also less likely to abuse substances such as alcohol and drugs, and as a result may experience better health. God, philosophy, horoscopes, and Pilates can provide frameworks that support you in asking large questions about your own life, beliefs, values, and honorability. Although some frameworks are more valuable than others.

THE FALL OF THE NEW GODS

In 2020, some of our twenty-first-century moral vectors began to crack and crumble. During the COVID-19 crisis, many observed how the public's stomach turned against the influencers, wellness gurus, and lifestyle celebrities we'd been devotedly following. Faced with such a stark physical reality, the dreams they offered of shiny skin, open hearts, and elevated auras began to feel vapid.

When life was (somewhat) stable, we'd glanced away from priests, ayatollahs, rabbis, imams, and prophets to the next largest figures in our eye line: celebrities. Of course, since the dawn of Hollywood we've looked to stars to tell us how to live, dress, and shop. But in recent years, as we've become divorced from spiritual leaders and disenfranchised from political ones, celebrities' roles as emotional compasses has swelled. They've taken central, sometimes instigating positions in social movements. After the election of Donald Trump—a man previously known to us through television and devoid of the practical experience to run a country—the public didn't cry out for a career public servant to save us. We begged Oprah to step in, run for president, and make the Oval Office truly mean something again. So complete was our trust in fame that we believed the only thing that could correct our overinvestment in one celebrity was overinvestment in another.

As it turns out, it's taken a global pandemic to wake us up to how freely we'd been handing out positions of moral authority. During the crisis global leaders struggled to communicate best safety practices and inspire a sense of unity and purpose. With places of worship already receded from our lives, there was a question of how we were to rally large groups around ideas of togetherness. In that vacuum, celebrities assumed it was up to them to step up. Movie, pop, and sports stars made DIY public service announcements instructing us to stay home, wash our hands, mask up, and look out for each other—sometimes from their palatial homes. While I, as much as anyone, mocked these stars freely, there was part of me that also thought: *We made them this way.* We elevated them so high above us because we were desperate for someone to tell us what to do.

It's very easy to sit at my desk and point out all the ways that searching for meaning in religion or religious proxies is flawed. But that dismisses the comfort that believing in something can provide. Our brains want to reject chaos by embracing narratives that let us feel we're not alone, that our pain exists for a reason. We want to believe our suffering isn't in vain—that it has value and is drawing us towards something worthwhile. I'm aware of the callousness, the smugness, of belittling that. As a kid, I might have been proud to glibly declare life meaningless. In adolescence God was easy to shrug off. But the older I get, the more I wonder if it's cruel to pry someone away from their concept of purpose.

My parents have both been handed seemingly endless menus of physical, emotional, and financial trials that I'm not sure I could have overcome. For them God, prayer, church, and doctrine are places of respite. Without that sanctuary, what's left? A spate of bad luck and a lot of pain? Pain, in the pursuit of *something*, is noble. Pain, in pursuit of nothing, is tragic.

That desire for eventual redemption is most apparent in ideas of an afterlife, a repeating feature of most major religions. When speaking of that space after death where we can experience total peace, they may call it heaven, paradise, moksha, or nirvana, but it's always a destination.

One to spend your whole life questing towards, a comfort for torment and a reward for goodness.

Newer systems of meaning express less directly the idea of a literal second place where we will finally be happy. But they're still built around motifs of journeys, transformations, and a drive to reach another state: one where we're gleaming, happy, beautiful, and well. The problem is that by placing such value in an afterlife, another point that exists in theory, we automatically devalue the present. Religions—whatever form they take, in whatever decade— may present a way to interrogate and understand our world. But they also remove us from it. They make existence, the pain and pleasure of it, a test to endure and move through.

We turn to wellness, celebrity worship, and thousand-dollar exercise bikes for meaning and comfort, but, for me, they still lead to the same knotty dilemmas: standards to be laid out, expectations that can't be met, and an overreliance on an external source to help us justify why each day is worth living. To resist that urge to grab onto something, but rather to face the infinite pointlessness of our lives, joys, anguish, and existence, is horrifying to many. It casts us totally adrift, alone. But it also marks us as completely free.

In the early months of COVID-19 we looked for meaning and reason: Why was this happening to us? What could we learn from it? What was it all for? Almost a year in, I don't ask those questions anymore. Without a true meaning to discover or another world to fixate on, I'm fully in my own body, mind, and life. When I stop looking for something else, I see the present clearly. With no higher power in control, no greater purpose in play, the responsibility to shape a good life falls to me alone. I resist the urge to ask others to tell me what's meaningful. I glance around and see for myself: What right now is beautiful, tasty, exciting, terrifying, unknowable? What makes my life feel precious, despite knowing it is ultimately pointless?

The answers I return with aren't big or complicated; they don't need to be contained within ideas of heaven or an afterlife. They're simple and small, and accessible right now. Today is the first day of spring. Yesterday my nephew turned ten. My boyfriend and our dog have begun to dress the same and right now that stupid fact brings me more joy than any promise of salvation. It is all meaningless; we're just bodies moving through space, careening towards no particular or vital ending. But does that matter? To me, no. Because I choose to see my life as something more than a trial to survive and endure. After all, it's all I have, the only one, and with that understanding, my pointless, ordinary existence becomes celestial.

THE DARK SIDE
OF NIHILISM

When this book was just a scramble of ideas, writing samples, and basic chapter outlines, my agent took it to a selection of publishers to see if anyone would be interested in working on it. Some people liked it, others didn't, but one publisher was appalled by the concept itself. They claimed that nihilism was such a dangerous perspective that to champion it at any time—but especially during a period so choked with apathy, greed, and destructive consumption—was reckless.

Obviously, I disagreed. But their revulsion and concern at the topic was an insight into how a lot of people feel about this kind of thinking. Criticisms of nihilism are understandable. As we've already discussed, across history a lot of dark stuff can be tied to it. Nazis, anarchists, and fatalists have all found refractions of themselves within its design, twisting and shaping it to speak to their own vile agendas.

That trend isn't confined to the past. Many of the most brutal and terrifying aspects of early twenty-first-century culture are still spun with meditations on meaningless-ness. Conspiracy theorists, incels, alt-right groups, and other hate-based movements regularly cherry-pick bits of nihilist philosophy to justify their abhorrent actions. So, when discussing nihilism and the ways it can, when man-aged carefully, be a deeply constructive presence in our lives, it's important to also explore why it lends itself so tidily to such disturbing realities.

By its nature, nihilism leaves a void where systems of meaning previously existed. There's a lot to gain by con-sidering that empty space. To accept a life without mean-ing is to re-examine your own understandings of worth, value, time, happiness, success, and connection. But it also poses risks, something Nietzsche himself understood. In *Beyond Good and Evil*, he wrote: "He who fights with mon-sters might take care lest he thereby become a monster. And if you gaze for long into an abyss, the abyss gazes also into you."

A void prompts an opportunity for reflection, but it's also a space that can be filled with whatever we want. Nihilism can serve as a funhouse mirror, reflecting and distorting our own beliefs. Approach it with pain and fear, and those feelings will be magnified. Go to it looking for a way to excuse gross behavior, and you'll find it.

While researching this chapter—descending into forums, publications, podcasts, and YouTube holes, exploring the darkest regions of nihilism and the cruel ways it can manifest—I was often surprised to see a version of my own beliefs mirrored back. At a glance, the individuals who held them were my total opposite. But the painful truth is that we share a root ideology—albeit one that led us down very different paths. If we're going to use nihilism as a constructive way to examine our lives, stare into the void, and not be consumed, that duality needs to be interrogated.

I was especially struck by the varied expressions of nihilism after the COVID-19 stay-at-home orders were imposed, as pockets of pandemic skeptics began organizing "freedom protests." These events were led and attended by a motley group of anti-vaxxers, wellness warriors, conspiracy theorists, and very scared and frustrated citizens. I didn't agree with the groups or their reasoning, but observing their shaky, front-facing camera phone monologues and Twitter manifestos, I recognized imprints in their arguments.

Writing this and fixating on the void means engaging in a lot of semiformed conversations about the inevitability of death and rejecting internalized ideas of reason, value, authority, power, and reality. Listening to COVID-19 skeptics talk about how the modern world is making us sick and sad while challenging people to face the brutality of existence, I heard some of the phrases I'd used myself.

There was one clip being shared around social media that I found particularly jarring. It featured an earth-tone-dressed, moonstone-adorned woman delivering a speech where she declared, "in this world you live until you die," and called on people to really live until they died. She argued that any attempt to deny the inevitable chaos of life—say by wearing a mask—was futile in the face of a universe that ultimately is just gonna do whatever it wants.

Looking at her, in her sun-flooded living room, windows open, with vaguely new-agey artwork in the background, it occurred to me that this woman was an existential nihilist. I showed it to my boyfriend and asked, "Is this what I sound like? If I'm also saying nothing really matters, am I that different from her?"

Watching the clip over my shoulder, he didn't share my concern, replying, "You're different because you're not an asshole." Staring back at her, eyes wide as she talked about her hopes that people would find a way to enjoy their lives, I wondered, *Is she an asshole though?* It felt more complicated than that.

The divide between people I agreed with and those I didn't, those who were soothed by nihilism rather than being consumed by it, couldn't just be a watery sense of internal morality. My journey led me to sunny nihilism, a space where I feel free but focused, see myself diminished, but inherently connected to those around me. She'd gone another way. Her path had turned toxic, making her indifferent to other people's lives and sure that our time on earth wasn't only pointless, but also worthless. Nihilism to me has been a revelation, a space where I can finally breathe. For others, the vacuum of meaning is crushing, a gaping hole so chilling, it leaves them vulnerable to exploitation, or invites them to become the exploiters themselves.

Nihilism's first wave at the close of the nineteenth century came during a period of tidal political, economic, social, and cultural change that saw people drastically reconsidering how they lived and viewed their lives. The philosophy suggested that historic ways of assigning meaning and purpose were not finite but flexible, able to be challenged, remade, and discarded.

Earlier in this book I laid out how we're uniquely primed for a return to nihilism. From the deepest recesses of the internet to parents at after-school pickup, people are looking at society and finding it lacking. They're losing faith in historic institutions, pushing back against media narratives, and challenging why systems and structures exist in the first place. Sometimes that's constructive. Questions like, *Why do I work like this, value the things I do, and absorb the expectations of others when they make me feel sapped and hollow?*, can be transformative. Other times it's insidious, eroding the foundations of a mostly fair and safe society, making it easier to also posit questions like, *Why must a president be honorable, a government be committed to the needs of the most vulnerable, or a journalist be protected from persecution?*

By his own description, Nietzsche "philosophized with a hammer," breaking open large ideas and challenging his readers to see what could be reformed with the pieces. But with cracks that wide, a lot can seep in.

Nietzsche has a history of being misread and misappropriated by dangerous groups. In the 1930s, fascists picked and chose from his work to back up their own cruelty and malice. Today he has again become an icon for some of the bleakest explorers of culture and life online. Almost a hundred years ago, Hitler fawned over Nietzsche's books; Richard Spencer, the neo-Nazi who claims to have coined the term "alt-right," proudly claims to have been "red-pilled" by him. In the *Vox* feature "The Alt-Right Is Drunk on Bad Readings of Nietzsche. The Nazis were too," Sean Illing argued: "For someone on the margins, stewing in their own hate or alienation or boredom, [Nietzsche's] books are a blast of dynamite. All that disillusionment suddenly seems profound, like you just stumbled upon a secret that justifies your condition."

When I read Nietzsche, I find he pries my exhausted brain from the fixations that taunt me: expectations of how my life should be, how others should see me, how I should feel, how my time should be spent. His work has led me to other authors such as Naomi Klein, Rebecca Solnit, and David Graeber, who have in turn also challenged me to ask why I value what I value, believe what I believe.

But reading Nietzsche or exploring nihilism from a more selfish or hateful perspective, there are a lot of burrs to catch on to. This philosophical hammer can be used to destroy any aspect of modern life you find restrictive or inconvenient, or that otherwise prevents you from doing whatever you like. Some individuals feel compelled to fill the space where meaning was with the ideas that serve them best. As Illing continues: "[Nietzsche] tells you that the world is wrong, that society is upside down, that all our sacred cows are waiting to be slaughtered. So if you're living in a multiethnic society, you trash pluralism. If you're embedded in a liberal democracy, you trumpet fascism. In short, you become politically incorrect—and fancy yourself a rebel for it."

Interestingly, what so many who read nihilism like this ignore is that Nietzsche expressly warned against these kinds of interpretations. While he was probably not the most charming man to sit next to on a train, he bristled at people's desire to define themselves by race, belief, or country; at those who flatten their identity and worldview to merge into any homogeneous mass who think, act, and follow orders just like them.

Nietzsche wasn't blind to how the broad strokes of nihilism opened it to interpretation and manipulation. He was frightened "by the thought of what unqualified and unsuitable people may invoke my authority one day. Yet that is the torment of every teacher . . . he knows that, given the circumstances and accidents, he can become a disaster as well as a blessing to mankind." He imagined and feared for a future where people filled the void at the heart of nihilism with their own needs and desires. But as insightful as he was, it's hard to imagine that when he was perforating the borders of what we're conditioned to believe, he'd have expected to create a rip that would see reality itself pour out.

In recent years, we've all witnessed the rapid rise of new and existing conspiracy theories. Family WhatsApp groups, social feeds, and even the floors of Congress have become choked with questionable opinions on the pandemic, technology, the environment, healthcare, politicians, and cultural leaders that previously would have felt too ridiculous for most people to utter out loud.

As an adult, I roll my eyes at mentions of new world orders and deep state conspiracies. But before they'd marbled mainstream life, inspired acts of violence, and threatened the institutions of power I have some lingering faith in, I was drawn to many of these ideas myself. In my teens I devoured books about cryptozoology, ancient aliens, the illuminati, and the occult. My interest was partly fantastical: I enjoyed them in the same way I liked horror movies or freaking out my friends with urban legends at sleepovers. But I also found it cathartic to look at the world as I knew it, and ask: *What else?*

Those strange stories offered an alternative roadmap of the world where things weren't what they seem. They also helped explain how people, who I wanted to believe were basically good, could treat each other in such awful ways. They lived in the part of my brain that now occupies itself with activism, critical thinking, leftist politics, questioning what I'm taught, and, yes, nihilism.

Working on this chapter, I spent a lot of time researching the major veins of conspiracy thinking that exist today.

Without doubt, the central line is QAnon: a collection of cobbled-together ideologies, fears, theories, hysterics, and bigotry that's so convoluted and complex it's difficult to explain without dedicating the rest of the book to it. But hell, I'll give it a go.

QAnon first surfaced in 2017 when an (at the time of writing) anonymous person (or persons), calling themselves "Q" and claiming to be a high-ranking official in the U.S. government, began posting cryptic messages on imageboard website 4chan. Early reports were largely political (pro Trump, anti Clinton), but over the years, QAnon's expansion has been fueled by how it weaves together existing conspiracies to create a shifting mass of ideas anyone can sew their own agenda into.

Broadly breaking down the group's current worldview in the *New York Times*, Kevin Roose explained: "QAnon is the umbrella term for a sprawling set of internet conspiracy theories that allege, falsely, that the world is run by a cabal of Satan-worshipping pedophiles who are plotting against Mr. Trump while operating a global child sex-trafficking ring . . . in addition to molesting children, members of this group kill and eat their victims in order to extract a life-extending chemical from their blood."

People used to make jokes about QAnon and their bizarre theories, but during 2020 their very real threat became clear. Followers have been linked to several alleged criminal acts, including multiple murders, kidnappings, and assaults. In 2019 the FBI called them "conspiracy theory-driven domestic extremists" and a growing domestic terror threat. The warning has done little to hamper their growth: The 2020 U.S. election saw Marjorie Taylor Greene, a vocal QAnon supporter, win the House seat representing Georgia's Fourteenth Congressional District. When a mob of thousands stormed the U.S. Capitol building on January 6, 2020, spurred on by President Trump and angry about his election loss to Joe Biden, many were spotted wearing QAnon insignia.

Sometimes when I read about QAnon, I try to imagine a set of circumstances where I (or my teen self) would join them. How disillusioned would I need to be with the world around me to engage in such a fractured alternative to it? I have no doubt that a shadow of nihilism leads people to these spaces. When they lose faith in one reality, become disconnected from the version of meaning being sold to them, they seek out another.

For me, nihilism invites a change of perspective, one that considers the expanse of the universe and our tiny place within it. Viewed with such scope, the curve of a river or the reach of a tree begin to feel as sweeping and impactful as our long, full lives. It's humbling to think about, but it's also kind of slow. There are no exciting plot twists, reveals, or crescendos. It's more like, *Relax, you're inconsequential, so go pat a dog or something.*

Conspiracy theories appeal to people who are also waking up to the idea that to the universe, to society, even to people in power who should be watching out for them, they don't matter. But rather than accept this, they grasp for an alternative narrative: one that doesn't say, "You don't matter," but rather that "No one matters as much as you." They remake the world into a place where the individual, as the witness to existence as it "truly is," is a holder of knowledge and power. In his 1964 *Harper's* essay "The Paranoid Style in American Politics," Richard Hofstadter wrote that the conspiracy theorist sees themselves as "always manning the barricades of civilization." They're the only one, or one of a few, who can create change, locate meaning, and act with purpose. At a glance, groups like QAnon may seem like the product of nihilism, but in a way they're an attempt to escape from it.

University of Melbourne social anthropologist James Rose explained that conspiracy theories thrive during stressful times because individuals' "existing idea systems have begun to break down under pressure and are no longer sufficient to explain what's going on around them." As individuals lose jobs, income, freedoms, their health, even the people they love, they seek out anything that can explain how "daily life has become so unpredictable."

For them, the idea that our lives can fragment for no reason beyond the cruel luck of the universe is more terrifying than the fantasy that we're under attack from a great enemy. They'd rather believe in a version of the world that's a nightmare, where leaders drink children's blood, than consider the nihilistic alternative. Better the meaning of life be horrifying than not exist at all.

My own experience of nihilism is, as demonstrated, pretty sunny. But that experience doesn't blind me to the fact that for a lot of people, considering that their life is pointless is terrifying and all consuming. It can't be shaken off with a glance outside or the suggestion they take a walk. I don't want to minimize how unbearably painful that feeling can be or suggest everyone should just get over it—because dismissing that pain can have chilling consequences. Nowhere is this more true than in twenty-first-century nihilism's most toxic and disturbing manifestation—the black pill community.

A VIOLENT VOID

Let's pause for a brief primer on what internet "pills" are. Put *very* basically, pills are online shorthand that describe an individual's worldviews. The reference comes from *The Matrix*—the internet's favorite movie—where the protagonist, Neo (Keanu Reeves), is presented two options by his soon-to-be mentor, Morpheus (Laurence Fishburne). Holding out a red and a blue pill, Morpheus explains the two routes ahead: Neo can "take the blue pill," which means staying in (the computer-generated) reality as he knows it, "the story ends; you wake up in your bed and believe whatever you want to believe." Or he can "take the red pill . . . stay in Wonderland and I show you how deep the rabbit hole goes." The red pill is effectively an awakening, the ability to see the world how it truly is. Spoiler alert: Neo takes the red pill and begins his journey into the "real" world.

Fast-forward twenty years, and blue pill thinking refers to people who choose to believe in the world as we're shown it: Life is fair and has meaning, an examined life is worth living, everyone is equal, the state is here to support you, follow the rules and you will be rewarded. Taking the blue pill signifies buying into myths of meaning and purpose and preached ideas of morality, consumerism, wealth, work, love, and so on.

Reading that, you could be tempted to see this book as an extension of red pill thinking, but personally I'd advise against it. While in theory, the red pill refers to moving from one belief system to another, being "red-pilled" has colloquially come to mean buying into the thinking of alt-right and misogynistic men's rights movements. It suggests life is corrupt and unfair, and challenges followers to rise up, reveal the lies, awaken others, fight for a correction of reality. What that action looks like can vary, from QAnon followers running for Congress to incels committing acts of extreme violence.

While there are seemingly endless "pill" variations, even reaching into environmentalism and feminism, they're most closely associated with incels, alt-right groups, and other pockets of extremist doctrine, especially the black pill. People who are "black-pilled" are often more passive, defeated, and nihilistic. They believe there is no point to anything, that their situation is permanent and inescapable, so their actions can't effect change. In short, no matter what, you're fucked. It's arguably the most extreme exhibition of nihilism: deeply rooted in misogynistic, bigoted, and often violent ideology, as well as rampantly self-destructive.

In her 2018 *Vox* article "What a Woman-Led Incel Support Group Can Teach Us about Men and Mental Health," Aja Romano wrote that these groups are "rife with depression, a nihilistic communal celebration of low self-esteem, and a widespread resistance to seeking therapy and getting treatment for mental illness." Many have called the black pill a death cult that advocates suicide, instructs people to "LDAR" (Lie Down and Rot), and preaches "going ER"—a chilling reference to Elliot Rodger. In 2014, Rodger—a misogynistic incel who blamed his problems on women not wanting to have sex with him—shot and killed six people in Santa Barbara, injured fourteen others, then turned the gun on himself. Since his attack, Rodger has become a dark hero figure, being referred to as "Saint Elliot" or "The Supreme Gentleman."

NIHILISTIC GRIFTERS

Nihilism of this kind can be violent and destructive, but it also creates an opening for others to exploit. When you're lost, looking for something to believe in, or mourning a loss of purpose, you begin to search for new heroes and villains. In his *Atlantic* article "The Conspiracy Theorists Are Winning," Jeffrey Goldberg calls the individuals who take advantage of this vulnerability "nihilistic grifters."

The most visible example is, of course, Donald Trump—a person so barren of personal values or morals he's easily able to absorb the fears, frustrations, hopes, dreams, and hatreds of others.

But he's not the only one to gain power from exploiting the disconnection of others. In his article, Goldberg presents conspiracy theorist and radio host Alex Jones as a prime example of someone gaming people's greatest fears and prejudices to build an audience. Jones has made a career of stoking people's distrust in systems of power and challenging their basic grasp on reality. One of the many cracked conspiracies he's propagated is the idea that the Sandy Hook massacre, the Oklahoma bombings, and the 9/11 terrorist attacks were fake. He's also claimed the government is controlling the weather, Bill Gates is a eugenicist with plans for global domination, and scientists are developing a "gay bomb" to, well, turn people gay.

Goldberg writes that these nihilistic grifters amass influence by "exploiting innocent people seeking to satiate the deep human need for coherence." Exploiting is right—this methodology handed Trump the presidency and has made Jones incredibly wealthy. The *New York Times* has reported that by 2014, Jones's "operations were bringing in more than $20 million a year in revenue," adding that Jones made most of his income "from the sale of products like supplements such as the Super Male Vitality, which purports to boost testosterone, or Brain Force Plus, which promises to 'supercharge' cognitive functions."

EMBRACING THE VOID, FOR GOOD

You don't have to fall so far down the rabbit hole to be destabilized by this kind of thinking; nihilism can still burrow into your brain and eat you alive without you submitting to online death cults. In my own life I often observe press coverage of nihilism gone wrong, and it's safe to say my social circle doesn't cross over into black-pilled incel groups too regularly. Most commonly it comes up regarding the question of whether to have children. It's one thing to say *life is meaningless, enjoy the memes, listen to a sad song, and get on with your day.* But when thinking about creating *new* life, you eventually have to reconcile with the value of *existing* life.

Arthur Schopenhauer argued that the point of existence, the meaning of life, was to create more of it. That impulse is coded into our very biology: the base desire for one cell to become two. But David Benatar, sometimes referred to as "the world's most pessimistic philosopher," disagrees. He is a leading voice in the anti-natalist movement, who believe life is so unbearable, full of such overwhelming and unavoidable pain, that it's unethical to subject a child to it at all.

In his book *Better Never to Have Been: The Harm of Coming into Existence*, Benatar explains: "While good people go to great lengths to spare their children from suffering, few of them seem to notice that the one (and only) guaranteed way to prevent all the suffering of their children is not to bring those children into existence in the first place."

I'm not sure if Benatar considers himself a nihilist, but he did tell the *New Yorker* he believes human life is meaningless, and the universe is undoubtedly indifferent to us: "I don't believe that suffering gives meaning . . . I think that people try to find meaning in suffering because the suffering is otherwise so gratuitous and unbearable."

I struggle to apply the math of pain and pleasure to my own existence (which, for the record, I do generally enjoy), and while it's no cosmic adventure, I'd say was worth being born for. Does every big bunch of fresh basil I smell make up for all the heartbreak I've suffered? Does the expanse and beauty of the ocean balance the pain of one day losing a parent? Will the joy I'll hopefully one day experience over the birth of my own child balance the carbon bomb his or her life will effectively detonate on our fragile planet? This is impossible to quantify. But reading Benatar's work, I always get stuck on the idea that we return to again and again: that the value of life is predicated on it "meaning" something.

Today the sun is shining. I had a good run this morning, in a few hours I'll eat something delicious for lunch, later I'll probably speak to someone I love. None of those actions are meaningful. No one will remember them after I die. I probably won't remember them in a week. They contribute nothing to the existence of the human race. But does that mean they weren't worth being born for?

To wish for meaning is to be devastated by its absence. To accept that life is meaningless but still full of pleasures that are better to exist for than not exist for, to me is personally a better bet. You can only fret over the lack of meaning if you allow yourself to buy into the myth of it at all.

Nietzsche saw nihilism as a state to move through. A blunt tool to dismantle existing ideas and assumptions, but then put down in the pursuit of something else. But exploring people's toxic experiences of it, it starts to feel like a bog you can't escape.

Despite Nietzsche's advice, nihilism isn't a temporary state for me—I choose to dwell in it full time. I view it as a life preserver, rather than a weight. That's not to say that embracing this kind of thinking is always easy. The thought that our lives effectively amount to nothing, our most ardent efforts effect little to no real change, and the universe is indifferent to our greatest joys and deepest sorrows is a lot to take in. I'm not a total thought-experiment cyborg—sometimes it all overwhelms me too. But I do believe that if we can embrace that fear, resist the urge to turn away and/or obscure it with reassuring (and endless) messages of easy-access purpose, we can find a kind of lasting comfort. It just takes a bit of practice.

Brushing my teeth yesterday morning, out of nowhere it hit me: *You're just going to die one day and that'll be it, all this will have been for nothing.* I felt a seizing terror for a moment before remembering, *Well, I won't be around to worry about it.* Walking through to my living room, I opened a window, leaned out, and reminded myself that I'd never get that moment back. It wasn't a particularly nice day: gray and rainy, with lashings of wind to tell me my hay fever would flare up soon. But as I looked across the alleyway to my neighbor sitting on her balcony, I thought about how rich and exciting her life probably was, how I'll never know it, how my whole street is overflowing with people and feelings, more than my brain could ever comprehend. The world in that instant seemed so full and lush it once again felt crazy to ask anything more from it. Sitting down at my desk to start the day, I felt better, my brain reordered.

Again and again while writing this, I've asked myself: *Why has my journey been so sunny while others' were so dark? If nihilism is a container that we put parts of ourselves in, why do others fill it with loneliness, fear, exploitation, greed, opportunism, and selfishness, while I place in it hope, community, beauty, pleasure, and peace?*

Part of it is luck: My life has not always been easy, but no doubt it has been easier than some others. Although I also think it's a mistake to see every violent person or toxic online space through a victim lens. I believe nihilism creates a fork in the road and we do have a choice which direction we take. In her aforementioned *Vox* article on black-pilled incels, journalist Aja Romano quoted one online moderator who reflected that leaning into this sense of pointlessness was liberating. "You can stop worrying about improving yourself, stop worrying about the years passing by and your chances getting slimmer, stop worrying about what will happen in the future, because you are certain of your place in the world and what is going to happen."

That statement is in some ways aligned with, but also the opposite of, my thinking. Nihilism states that nothing matters. It levels existing hierarchies of how we spend our time and assign value. That idea leads some to ask: Why do anything at all? If there's no ultimate payoff, why play the game? This never entirely made sense to me. I don't understand why something not having a huge purpose devalues all the small pleasures embedded within it. It's like saying: *I know each meal I partake in will eventually end, so I choose to eat nothing.*

Nihilism to me shifts focus from "the end" to create space in our lives for the "right now." If there is no meaning or final reward, all we have is our life as it exists today. In many ways, all philosophy is about considering a "void." It's human to automatically try to fill it with new values, messages, leaders, rewards, or ourselves. But if we can accept that empty space, not allow it to be a hole in our lives through which to fall, I believe we can find a kind of relief.

SUNNY NIHILISM
FOR EVERYDAY LIFE

n a 2020 *New York Times* profile of Canadian-American astronomer and planetary scientist Sara Seager, journalist Chris Jones observed that, for astrophysicists, "knowing that there are hundreds of billions of galaxies and that each might contain hundreds of billions of stars" can make their lives "and even those closest to them seem insignificant." Seager's work is focused on the search for exoplanets—planets orbiting a star other than our sun that may support life.

Understandably, viewing existence with such an epically wide gaze can sometimes leave Seager feeling detached from the terrestrial goings-on around her. Moving through life, so conscious of her own smallness and the smallness of others, she has difficulty connecting with the banal necessities of her own existence. What do small talk, grocery lists, or social niceties mean when you understand that everything is meaningless in the scope of the universe? As a result, Seager can sometimes appear to be something of an alien herself: inhabiting the world, while also somewhat separate from it.

Observing this, Jones writes, "Astrophysicists are forever toggling between feelings of bigness and smallness, of hubris and humility, depending on whether they're looking out or within." A version of that sense of bigness and smallness, hubris and humility, can also be found when considering nihilism—it's what so many of us fear about it. We worry that by embracing meaninglessness our minds will be reformed like Seager's, that we will become detached and despondent, divorced from the things we love and want to believe matter so much.

Sunny nihilism offers a different result. Rather than leaving you feeling disconnected and deadened, embracing sunny nihilism means becoming more mindful and open to the pleasures of your pointless, forgettable, insignificant existence.

Viewed like that, with humility at the core instead of isolation, nihilism shifts from a terrifying concept to a soothing one. An awareness of our own insignificance displaces us from the center of our own lives and challenges us to review what matters if we don't.

The "bigness" that nihilism highlights is understandable. Everyone from astronomers to stoners has at some point marveled at the inconceivableness of the universe and their inconsequential place within it. But day to day, it's easy to lose sight of the scale of our problems, aspirations, disappointments, and grievances. Left unchecked they can see us swell in our own minds until we start to feel like planets everyone else is merely orbiting.

In contrast to this, sunny nihilism slips in, reminding you that not only will you not be remembered, but every great human, action, thought, and moment will eventually be washed away. Spend a while thinking like this, and you'll notice a strange transformation occur. While we ourselves may feel dwarfed by the scope of a forever-reaching cosmos, the smallest elements of life begin to expand. If nothing actually matters, focus and priorities shift to *this* moment. We understand that the present, however mundane, is as fleeting, temporal, fragile, and ultimately forgettable as the greatest events in human history. The world contracts to be as small as the second we find ourselves in.

Approached this way, nihilism moves from demoralizing to freeing. It makes you wonder about what you do and don't give your attention to. Is what another person thinks of us as meaningful (or meaningless) as a brush of lilac tumbling over a neighbor's fence? Seen from a sunny nihilist's perspective, no. So why do we allow ourselves to be consumed by one while ignoring the other? Both are, after all, just an absurd sequence of random events, happening for no reason at all, that will exist once and then be gone.

This talk of the bigness and smallness of life is easy enough to digest on clear days, when the laundry is done and work is going well. But the (unfortunate) reality is that your life is probably built around medium-level concerns. These include, but are not limited to: jobs, fate, destiny, ego, what others think of you, anxiety about the future, expectations of what a relationship should be, and opinions about purpose. They're the knotty concepts we create, cling to, and try to control. That most of us invest in and assign meaning to, in the hope they will bring clarity, relief, and happiness.

HOW MEANING MAKES YOU SELFISH

From the moment we wake up and decide whether to snooze our alarms or get out of bed, we begin drawing in medium-sized decisions about how we want to live. Every moment of every day is in part dedicated to these choices and the promise that maybe they will deliver comfort and ease. Medium-level concerns span a wide range of topics. Each of us will have a different set and experience them differently. But for the most part, said decisions (along with all the systems of meaning explored in this book) have one thing in common: They generate a swirl of ideas and ideals that allow us to place ourselves at the center of everything. How *we* feel, what *we* want, the experiences *we've* had or wish to have, what *we* find meaningful.

But the reality is, in a society of single units that worships individualism, where our own well-being is seen as separate from others' and everyone is clamoring for their own slice of happiness, the quest for personal meaning often sets us at odds with each other. In his book *Can We Be Happier? Evidence and Ethics*, labor economist Richard Layard worries about this cult of the individual meaning: "In modern culture the selfish strand is now legitimized as never before. The chief goal on offer to young people is success relative to others—better grades, higher pay, more friends, and greater fame. Increasingly, young people compete in every possible avenue of life." This en masse search for happiness, carried out alone, with our own needs in mind, has hardly resulted in a uniform pod of elevated emotional beings. Rather, it has delivered a heritage of endless competition, dissatisfaction, and isolation as we all scramble for a piece of a poisoned pie.

This slow spread of selfish enlightenment has been a well-engineered effort, so you can't feel too bad about falling prey to it. Who hasn't read a listicle about nondemanding environmental actions to take at home that just happened to be paid for by a bank that invests in fossil fuels? Or flipped through a cookbook that frames the purchase of thirty-dollar olive oil as a "radically tender" act? It's not uncommon for me to get seven minutes into an influencer livestream about "community," "holding space," or "really seeing each other" before I realize they've been talking about themselves the whole time.

We've been taught to behave like this; shaped by the knocks of a capitalist culture that has not only privatized economies and industry, but also our sense of self. In modern life, happiness is a solitary mission, defined by what we see through our own windows. Mark Zuckerberg, a man as responsible as anyone for the proliferation of this narrow vision, once defended Facebook's algorithm, designed as it is to mirror and reinforce our own perspectives, by suggesting that "a squirrel dying in your front yard may be more relevant to your interests right now than people dying in Africa." It's a chilling observation, but one that demonstrates how a species nourished by community, connection, and solidarity has been conditioned to observe itself as separate.

Zuckerberg didn't create this reality alone though. Almost every area of our lives carries the same message: You are special, unique, central, important. Cosmetics brands insist we're all individuals, a fact that can only be celebrated through products that make us look like everyone else. Companies existing within the gig economy offer cheap and convenient services at the expense of the safety and livelihood of those delivering them. We accept this because we believe we're uniquely deserving. Our precious, meaningful time can't be wasted. Algorithms and cookies turn social media into a digital replica of our brains, an online reality where we are always right and our interests are always central.

In her collection of short essays *Intimations*, Zadie Smith muses about the work of writers, and how "they take this largely shapeless bewilderment and pour it into a mold of their own devising." She's reflecting on how writers bend and construct realities, shifting what people say and do to form tidier narratives, make more concise points, locate purpose more fluidly. But that instinct can also be applied to our compulsion to stuff meaning into every crevice of our lives. When we consider an existence with no inherent point, we rush to create one. We fill that void with our own desires, values, jobs, hobbies, relationships, gods, and ourselves.

As established, the search for meaning, in theory, is a noble pursuit, one that asks us to interrogate our choices, the treatment of others, what we value and prize, what we condemn and dismiss. Many people seek meaning through the service of others, the creation of art, the protection of nature. Most religions preach humility, poverty, taking responsibility for your fellow humans. But glancing around, how often do we truly see those values in practice?

If we're truly honest, more commonly the pursuit of meaning is selfish. It's an opportunity to obsess over ourselves, to reroute the whole world directly to us. A belief in our own specialness allows us to welcome a reality where our needs and feelings are the supreme priority, where agonizing over our appearance, purpose, moods, sleep patterns, and diet isn't obnoxious or self-obsessed. Instead, all this anointing and fawning over our minds, bodies, lives, and habits is elevated to a near-religious act.

GETTING OVER YOURSELF

You'd hope that all this self-obsession would at least result in a level of pleasure. But the kicker is that the search for meaning through the endless examination and worship of ourselves is only making us feel worse.

Which brings us to one of the central challenges to any sunny nihilist: asking, *What if I'm not special?* To gaze at a world carefully engineered by advertising, technology, religion, love, jobs, and our parents to make us feel central and unique, and admit we are, just like everything else, meaningless.

After a lifetime spent in a strange diorama of self-obsession, you'd think that facing your own pointlessness would be an existentially traumatizing process. But it doesn't have to be. Ironically, in a reality constructed to make us feel significant, but which more often leaves us anxious and miserable, this reminder of our own insignificance offers a strange sense of peace. Admitting that in the span of all time our presence is meaningless eases fixations on legacy, ego, and purpose, allowing us to shift focus from "one day" to the immediate moment, and take pleasure in the random existence we were wildly lucky to be gifted at all. But beyond offering a mindful break, or a check-in with our chronic self-obsession, this reduction of self leads to other deliberations. Namely, what do you do with the part of your brain that was formerly so singularly occupied with yourself?

Unfortunately the belief that nothing matters doesn't free you from the need to participate in the exchanges of time, money, and energy that make a society a society and not just a scramble of philosophers walking around wondering who is going to make lunch. So, when pondering how to spend said time, money, and energy, sunny nihilism leads you to ask: *If I don't matter, and am therefore not the center of everything and the priority, then what is? If I will be forgotten and lost to time, what will be remembered, at least for a little while?*

The American poet Walt Whitman asked something similar in his 1882 collection *Specimen Days & Collect*, written during and in the aftermath of the Civil War. He posed the question: "After you have exhausted what there is in business, politics, conviviality, love, and so on—have found that none of these finally satisfy, or permanently wear—what remains?" For Whitman, the answer was nature. He recognized it as something so much larger than himself that deserved the love and attention he might otherwise pour into more insular pursuits.

For each person, the answer is different. Personally, I'm with Whitman. Like many people of my generation, accepting the futility of my small life led me to deepen my commitment to environmentalism. Understanding that the only constant (at least until it's absorbed by the sun in a few billion years) is the Earth itself, its protection becomes more important than any singular interests of mine.

I'd encourage you to try the exercise for yourself. If you accept that you don't matter, that your name, ego, reputation, family, friends, and loves will soon be gone, how does the way you understand your own time, money, and energy change? Maybe the process reframes your attention to things you hope will last for a little longer than yourself: nature, art, culture, institutions, and causes you believe will benefit generations who've long forgotten your name. Or perhaps the question draws you back to that present moment: the small pleasures you can access today, the people you love, their right to feel safe, respected, well, and heard.

The suggestion to prioritize ideas and choices that benefit the world at large, as opposed to yourself in the moment, is central to the teaching of most major religions and several philosophical practices. But when mulling over how the rejection of individualism can make the planet (and ourselves) kinder and more reasonable, you can't go past the work of eighteenth-century German philosopher Immanuel Kant. I just want to pause to note that while Kant's work is relevant to themes explored here, the man himself was deeply problematic. His work was threaded with colonialist and racist thinking that sits at odds with his own writing on universal morality. When examining his theories today it's vital to not erase that reality to benefit a tidier narrative.

But we can consider some of his broad examinations in this context. Working during the Enlightenment and observing the retreat of religion in public and private life, Kant was interested in secular laws of universal morality. He believed that society needed a social code that could encourage people to treat each other well without the looming presence of God, heaven, and hell. In his 1785 book *Groundwork of the Metaphysics of Morals*, he introduced the "categorical imperative," which advised: "Act only according to that maxim by which you can at the same time will that it should become a universal law." At its most basic, the categorical imperative echoes the familiar advice to treat others as you'd like to be treated. But it also urges us to disengage from our individualistic perspective, to see all behavior as existing as part of a collective. Before making a choice or action, Kant pretty much advises you to ask: Is this behavior good or bad for society? If everyone were to act like this, would it be making things better or worse?

Kant was not a nihilist; he died sixty years before the term was even popularized. But Kantianism and nihilism are similar in how they drive us to understand existence as being so much bigger than ourselves. Approached right, this scale can be seen as more inspiring than crushing.

Nietzsche and Kant are long-dead white men whose lives looked drastically different from our own. But evidence of their ideas in action can be found everywhere at the present moment. While nihilism in the twenty-first century has in the experience of some continued to be a place to explore pain and anger, it's also been a rallying call to embrace a kind of radical selflessness. We've already looked at how a feeling of pointlessness is endemic in the lives of young people. And while the presence of incels and black-pilled online communities is impossible to ignore, so is the way this diminishment of self has led to a growing liberal-minded social shift—one that's less fixated on individual security, but demands a fairer, safer, and kinder world that benefits the broader population.

A LIFE MORE OR LESS ORDINARY

In her book *A Paradise Built in Hell*, Rebecca Solnit examines the way groups come together during crises, often displacing the selfish and separate impulses capitalism has pressed into them for a more united view of their community. Across earthquakes, wars, disasters, and accidents she catalogues people's expansive capacity for selflessness and altruism, observing, "When all the ordinary divides and patterns are shattered, people step up—not all, but the great preponderance—to become their brothers' keeper."

A Paradise Built in Hell largely looks at natural disasters and freakish man-made accidents. For countless people, our current century has felt like a rolling collection of such catastrophes. But time and time again, within the chaos, we've seen a new generation of nihilists step up and "become their brothers' keeper." As systems that formerly offered meaning have eroded, individuals haven't crumbled with them. And while innumerable numbers of us have watched aspirations around employment, home ownership, and financial security dim, we've taken the opportunity to challenge the status quo all together, rather than attempt a last-chance grab for ourselves.

For those championing issues such as (but not limited to) racial justice, real climate solutions, the end of police violence, and investment in secure housing, priorities are firmly fixed on the populace over the individual. By challenging and dismantling existing structures that may in some cases personally serve us, we're throwing away fantasies of our own importance to allow space for new ideas that reach further than our own front yards. From that perspective, riding a bike, recycling, investing money in clean banks and retirement funds, voting against high-income tax breaks, attending protests over work, passing up jobs in well-paying but morally dubious industries, and calling out sexism, racism, and classism in private spaces are in a way acts of sunny nihilism. Ones we partake in not because they make us happy, but because we know our happiness alone ultimately doesn't matter. If we are pointless, so are our selfish pursuits.

This expression of personal dissolution has been on display in many of our communities during the COVID-19 pandemic. As cases around the world began to spike, and whole cities became obsessed with daily rates, graphs, predictions, and curves, several of us likely witnessed an evolution take place. At first, the virus made us hyperaware of ourselves: Everything we touched or that touched us was a possible infection point that might introduce the disease into our body, disrupting or even ending our lives. But as the days went on, that awareness evolved.

At the beginning of the outbreak my apartment building started a WhatsApp group and people chatted on it day and night about serious news and mundane occurrences. We implicitly seemed to understand that we were living and moving through this crisis as a collective, only ever as safe as each other. Our previous compartmentalized private lives were an illusion allowed through luck and fragile health. Now, all choices and actions were shared experiences. When we washed our hands, we did it for ourselves, but also for the neighbors we shared door handles with.

Outside our building's walls that sentiment played out across the city at large through the rise of the organized and informal mutual aid networks that ribbon through neighborhoods. Food pantries dotted streets where local kids deposited spare fruit and vegetables from their gardens. People out of work held fundraisers for others worse off than themselves. Social media pivoted away from gentle bragging to become a public message board sharing health notices and offers of support and solidarity.

Of course, it would be naive (and arguably delusional) to suggest this community spirit was a universal response. Not surprisingly, as the crisis dragged on, surging and receding in waves, many slunk back to their old ways. The collective spirit and unity of the early months dulled as our fear splintered into boredom, frustration, blame, and anger.

COVID has behaved like nihilism: It has driven some into the darkest parts of themselves. It has made others aware of the right now and the eternal, forcing them to live in the moment: *How do I feel right now? Is my mask fitted correctly? Are my hands clean?* But it has also demanded we consider the scope of our lives like never before: *What will be left at the end of this? What will matter then? How will history write about us?*

It's difficult, writing this in the middle of this awful pandemic, to know if the cult of the individual has been permanently altered. After all, humans have been trying to pry themselves away from these singular ideas for centuries. In the thirteenth century, the poet Rumi warned of the anguish a lone outlook brings, writing: "You're clutching with both hands to this myth of 'you' and 'I.' Our whole brokenness is because of this." Instead, he urged readers to live "As if you and I have never heard of a you and an I."

Omid Safi is an American professor of Asian and Middle Eastern Studies at Duke University in North Carolina who specializes in Rumi as well as Islamic mysticism (Sufism). Speaking on *Vox*'s *Future Perfect* podcast, he reflected on the poet, and on what Sufi teachings can offer us during confusing times. Observing how people are quick to "think that we end at the edge of our fingertips," he counters that instead we remember we're fluid beings, our souls already "extending and enmeshed with other people." With these ideas in mind, Professor Safi proposes an alternative "ego annihilation" that rejects the concept of a self separate from others and instead accepts "one life, one soul, one yearning, one living, one love." It's only then, he posits, that "the pain and the suffering that we might witness in somebody else, and our own pain and suffering, might resonate with one another."

Thoughts of nihilism don't traditionally sit comfortably alongside poetry, mysticism, or meditations on the resilience of the human spirit. But examined together they arrive at a similar conclusion: Fixating on yourself is meaningless.

THE SWEET RELIEF OF NIHILISM

People subscribe to systems of meaning for countless reasons, and it's naive to suggest that in one book (or lifetime) we could ever understand why people pray, obsess over their jobs, dream of love, or allow themselves to be converted by conspiracies. But it's not foolish to say people searching for meaning are also looking for threads of happiness, peace, and connection. Whether it's at church or on an Instagram live stream, we're all reaching for relief.

In 2019 I profiled *New Yorker* writer Jia Tolentino ahead of the release of her earth-quaking essay collection *Trick Mirror: Reflections on Self-Delusion.* The book touches on several of these themes, and it's probably not surprising that our conversation turned towards nihilism and its capacity for good. She admitted to finding feelings of insignificance "really galvanizing," adding: "If we're here for just a blink of the eye, and in general if nothing matters, it feels like [it's] carte blanche to wild the fuck out. To try a lot of things, try your best to do something because the odds are so good that none of it means anything that perversely it makes me feel free to try."

Freedom is something most of us contemplate and covet. It sits alongside meaning as one of the most alluring and elusive prizes for a life lived "right." It's also one of the truest rewards for embracing nihilism, its deepest pleasure. Skeptics of nihilism fear it results in a freedom to indulge in destructive selfishness. But in reality, sunny nihilism is a chance to untether yourself from structures that dictate what we should think, feel, value, and desire. A partner who doesn't meet our every constructed, romantic expectation isn't a failed Heathcliff, but rather just another random collection of atoms who happens to sometimes make us laugh. A missed opportunity at work isn't a signal that we are subpar humans. It's a marker of time and power another person is attempting to place on us, one that we can shrug off, understanding that in the gaping abyss of the universe, it, like all things, is meaningless.

In both cases, our finite time is better spent elsewhere, enjoying pleasures that are real, not imagined. Personally, I like patting my dog, going for a walk, or eating something delicious. Either way, a dip into nihilism leaves us free to not only live our lives, but enjoy them. Because while the search for meaning is supposed to open up the world to us, help us understand others and ourselves, too often our meaningful fixations end up removing our ability to actually do this. We want to believe that meaning enriches and elevates our actions, but more regularly an injection of meaning just impress them with the need to "have a point."

My boyfriend is a commercial artist who also does university lecturing work. During lockdown his weekly classes were relocated to Zoom, offering me the surprisingly enjoyable experience of witnessing him in action from my neighboring home desk. In one class he encouraged his students to incorporate an element of play into their practice, to ensure they had time to experiment and make art for themselves that no one would ever see, judge, or reward them for. He stressed that this time was as vital as their graded or billable hours, as it not only allowed them to develop their style, but also ensured they'd maintain a relationship to this beloved process that was removed from work. To me this sounded like good advice, but the clear discomfort of the students was jarring. Again and again they asked him how this direction related back to final assignments and future grades. Not only were they confused by the direction towards pointless pleasure, but clearly distressed by it.

I'm sure many of us relate to the students' discomfort. What my boyfriend saw as freedom, they saw as pointlessness, a meaningless drain on their important, quantifiable time, which would be better spent in the pursuit of a "meaningful" goal, like getting a letter grade no one would ask about in six months' time. The "pointless" goal of trying to enjoy their work seemed absurd—which is honestly fair. Pointlessness is a state we've been conditioned to distrust. Competitive and destabilized structures of employment, parental pressure, student debt, skyrocketing living costs, and regressive markers of success like buying a house have loaded most of us with a bottomless sensation of always being behind on what we *should* be doing in pursuit of a "good life." In the scramble to make up time, we try to supercharge every action to be as meaningful as possible. Everything we do needs a point, a focus, a goal, in an attempt to serve as one more step towards a level of happiness and success.

But, as this book argues, it's a false promise. The breathless pursuit of most "meaningful" achievements tends to leave you stressed, exhausted, disappointed, and frustrated. So, when "finding a point" makes you miserable, an alternative emerges: embracing the pleasure of pointlessness.

The first time nihilism brought me real relief was when I was walking home from work after a long and overwhelming day. I was stressed, exhausted, and anxious over the knowledge that the evening offered no respite. Emails would continue to tumble all night, making sleep feel not only impossible but also like a betrayal to my future self who would wake up to a toxic inbox. As the familiar rise of a panic attack began to swell, I tried to control my breathing, hoping to avoid adding *passed out in the street* to my list of personal concerns. I was bent over, hands on knees, when I first thought, "Who cares, one day I'll be dead and no one will remember me anyway." I immediately felt better.

That would-be-brutal refrain has since become a go-to motto. In another setting, those words are the barbed epithets of a toxic spiral. But paired with a commitment to meaninglessness, they puncture my own distorted and grotesque sense of self. Remembering your insignificance can be a sweet, freeing relief.

It's worth pausing for a moment to admit that all this embracing of pointlessness can be simpler to read (or write) about than actually do. Nihilism in general is easier to think about when the weather's good, our loved ones are well, and the news isn't too scary. But these perspectives are undeniably more complex for individuals living with loss, or whose bodies are threaded by pain and illness. When life feels fragile, most of us are less open to thought experiments about the meaninglessness of existence. Because the thing about nihilism, no matter how sunny, is that ultimately it requires a lot of thinking about death. Tangling with the emptiness of life means also accepting the empty finality that one day it will end.

Even people who don't dream of reincarnation, an afterlife, or absolution seek out forms of meaning in the hope it will make the thought of death bearable. There's comfort in the idea that our lives had a point, that we lived them right, did what we were supposed to do, checked the assigned boxes. But confronting death and meaninglessness doesn't need to be brutalizing.

When I'm overwhelmed, remembering that one day I won't exist makes whatever's stressing me appear small. In brighter moments, when I'm especially pleased with myself, the prompt that one day my body will disappear punctures my inflating ego. But even on the most ordinary days, the acceptance of finality transforms whatever bland environs I'm ignoring into an overwhelming buffet of smells, sights, and experiences that suddenly feel impossibly rare.

This "mindfulness of death" is central to the work of artificial intelligence scientist and Buddhist teacher Dr. Nikki Mirghafori. She's long been interested in our quest to escape death—whether it's through biohacking our bodies, searching for meaning, or clutching to belief systems that assure us death is not the end. But instead of avoiding thoughts of the brevity of life, Dr. Mirghafori suggests that accepting our own mortality and facing life's impermanence can align the way we live with our truest values. She points out that our lack of interest in contemplating how precious and fleeting our lives are allows us to waste them. Our ability to doomscroll, mindlessly binge TV, and participate in activities we don't find enriching or rewarding is fueled by how successful we have been at disconnecting from the idea that time is finite, our lives limited.

To help people confront their fear of death and experience the strange wonder that can come from that, Dr. Mirghafori suggests we try meditating with the mantra "this could be my last breath." The theory is that by doing so, we work through the terror a little at a time, by observing what comes to the surface during the practice and confronting each fear until we eventually reach a place of peace.

I can report that this is a terrifying exercise. At first it feels silly, like most meditation sessions. But once you start to settle in, sit with it, breathe in and out, a change occurs. Things move from silly to suffocating as you become aware of what you're actually telling your brain. It's almost like rehearsing your final moments, inviting your mind to flood with fear, regret, longing, loss, love, and gratitude. When you imagine each breath to be your last, each breath becomes a gift on arrival. Even after you're done, it's impossible to not enter the rest of your day with a degree of elation at being alive. The mantra evokes a sensation similar to examining nihilism: leaving you feeling lucky, ordinary, fragile, invisible, tender, and boundlessly grateful for even the painful parts of the day.

Epicurus once said: "Death does not concern us, because as long as we exist, death is not here. And when it does come, we no longer exist." It's a nicer version of the bratty, "Who cares, one day I'll be dead," but also a foundational concept of his philosophy and vision of how life should be experienced. Epicurus didn't believe in life after death, as either a punishment or reward. He taught that life and all it could offer was happening to us right now. Just as nihilism has become associated with narrow-minded destruction, his name is synonymous with hedonism and a ceaseless pursuit of selfish pleasures. But in reality, Epicurus was certain this kind of living would usher people away from materialism and greed. His pleasure principle championed being and doing good, arguing that with one precious life to enjoy, not a moment should be wasted in guilt or anxiety over pain caused to others. The only way to feel truly good was to treat people well.

Around 307 BCE Epicurus bought a house with a garden outside of Athens and established what today we'd probably call a commune, where he could see these theories put into practice. The specifics of the space are lost to time, but it's believed that followers of his work lived simply and communally there, sharing ideas, pursuing their interests, being close to nature, and generally reflecting on the value of friendship—something Epicurus was very into.

We can't know for sure what the garden was like, although it's easy to picture it as heaven on earth. But his and Dr. Mirghafori's suggestion that sitting with death, fragility, and temporary states can lead to fulfillment can be evidenced elsewhere. In her *Atlantic* essay "Surrendering to Uncertainty," writer Heather Lanier unpacks how the experience of raising a very ill child has changed her outlook: "I fiercely loved a baby I could lose in a number of horrifying ways. But the tenderness I felt offered up its own wisdom. *Don't squander this*, it said. *You want with all your might to wish this away. But there is something vital here, in all this unknown. It will teach you why you are truly alive.*" Lanier admits that before her daughter was born, she carried the same values and aspirations as many of us: "I thought I was alive to be perfect, to achieve awards, accolades, victories." But caring for someone "who would never breeze past developmental milestones. It would be a huge feat if she could learn to chew her food," transformed all that. Her experience with her daughter created a change in her. Being so close to life's fragility "unearthed an aching tenderness." It led her to reconsider her "previously held beliefs about what's important, and what makes life worth living" and brought her to a personal revelation that "Everything is transitory. Nothing is certain."

It's strange writing about pointlessness and how nothing means anything, because writing—like so many parts of life—is focused on getting to the point and reaching a conclusion. But sunny nihilism celebrates the opposite: the acceptance of a kind of open-ended chaos. Andy Warhol once said, "The more you look at the same exact thing, the more the meaning goes away, and the better and emptier you feel." He was talking about his purposely pointless art that still speaks so deeply to something within us that it routinely sells for tens of millions of dollars. But despite his example, emptiness is not a sensation many of us hurry to cultivate. In the search for meaning, we stuff our lives full of stimuli, messages, reason, rules, and expectations. We look for meaning and conclusions to be able to get to the end of a task, an art show, an essay, a life and say: This is the value. This is the point.

But the point sunny nihilism makes is that there is no point—to this chapter, this book, this life. Instead, embracing it calls you to discover the pleasure to be found in emptiness, in the void. It is at once a very simple and an impossibly complex request. One that asks so little of us, beyond a total reordering of how we see success, existence, death, and ourselves.

THE PLEASURE OF
POINTLESSNESS

History, family, culture, religion, and sandwich boards have long told us that the pursuit of meaning will enrich our lives, fill us with purpose, and make the daily grind a little easier to bear. But amid that promise it's worth pausing to ask: How many people actually feel like that? For all the talking, reading, thinking, debating, and fighting we do about meaning, who goes home at the end of the day, looks at themselves in the mirror, and sees a person who confidently grasps the meaning of their own life?

In reality, our twenty-first-century relationship to meaning and purpose has less to do with enlightenment and peace and more to do with crushing expectations and bottomless self-obsession. We inject meaning into everything, from housework to facials, and gorge on the resulting, if artificial, sense of purpose. As Virginia Heffernan, author of *Magic and Loss: The Internet as Art*, mused to *Politico*: "The recent fantasy of 'optimizing' a life—for peak performance, productivity, efficiency—has created a cottage industry that tries to make the dreariest possible lives sound heroic."

Lost inside this fantasy, every waking moment is interrogated and performed. It becomes impossible to even make your bed without first asking: *Why am I doing this? What does it mean? What does it say about me? How is it feeding into my glorious future?* It's exhausting. We are all exhausted. And we are exhausting each other. So why do we keep doing it? Why do we partake in all this searching, stretching, and inventing of meaning—even when it only adds to our unease? We do so because the alternative is even more distressing. To reject meaning, and embrace that we don't matter (and neither does anything else), is to face the inevitable and infamous *void*.

The void can present and feel different to each person. For some it's a sense of pointlessness, a deep loneliness, a terror of death. However it appears, the response is usually the same: We scramble to fill it. Rather than face our own meaninglessness, we create or buy into systems that tell us we absolutely *do* matter. Whether you pick religion, love, work, ego, attention, money, fame, or any other value currency, you're practicing the same act of self-preservation—resisting the abyss. We're all so afraid that if we don't partake in the quest for meaning something terrible will happen. An acceptance of the pointlessness of life will consume us. Rot us from the inside out. Turn us into the familiar specter of a black-pilled, toxic nihilist.

So we scamper back from the void, or at least try to fill it by loading every interaction and moment with apparent purpose. But there is an alternative option: leaning deeper into the dark, accepting that *yes* we will eventually disappear and be forgotten, which frees us from the systems of meaning that work so hard to distract and console, but ultimately mostly exhaust. The ones that may buffer us from our most immediate fears, but also prevent us from fully embracing that our lives are pointless, fragile, precious, and dazzling things.

Sunny nihilism is a way for us to wrestle with this by reframing focus onto the biggest and smallest parts of our lives. It says you don't matter, your life is pointless, it's not leading to any great meaning or revelation. With this resolve outlooks shift. The smallest subjects balloon, the largest recede, and innumerable topics that usually occupy the majority of our energy begin to seem ridiculous. When we say, "nothing matters," that we have one life that will be over too soon and then forgotten, our attention migrates to the right now. The only thing that feels truly real is the present, not the projection of what could be, what might exist one day.

THIS IS, UNAVOIDABLY, IT

Sometimes when I'm on runs that are going badly, where my mind is scattered and my body not cooperating, I tell myself, "This day will never exist again. After this, it's gone, you've lost it." Instead of being swept away by the current of endlessly passing, never-replaceable time, I become awake to the preciousness of such a pointless (and even uncomfortable) moment. I notice the way the gum trees fringe the river, the cutting smell of eucalyptus and how it changes throughout the year.

Such talismans are locatable in our lives. Next time you eat a delicious peach, stare at the face of someone you love, or laugh at a perfect joke, try to step back and consider the act as a sunny nihilist. Remind yourself that this instant exists for no reason, it is in many ways a cosmic mistake, a fluke. But one that you were lucky enough to come across. It will make a sweet, passing second feel like the greatest gift of your life. Which—like all passing seconds that exist at random then dissolve forever—it is.

CREATING A MEANINGLESS LIFE

Chances are, these are skills many of us have already begun to refine during the COVID-19 pandemic. Times of crisis and fear have a tendency to make us see our lives clearly, allowing us to identify the big and small issues more easily than when things are going well. When we're sad, we have an acute understanding of what used to make us happy. When we're lonely, we know exactly who we love and miss. When we're deprived, we have no doubts about what we value.

My hometown of Melbourne carried out one of the longest and strictest lockdowns in the world. It was terrible, but also illuminating. So many spaces where I previously looked for meaning appeared suddenly barren. My interest in a career waned, while I became engrossed in new pursuits that had previously felt like a waste of time. I dedicated a lot of energy to the care and maintenance of my small balcony, growing jasmine and lavender to feel closer to my mother and her garden, neither of which I was able to visit. It was vital that I held on to my job and I respected the people who gave it to me, but there was nothing it could offer me that would feel anywhere near as good as stretching out on my parents' lawn—an act that I might have previously declared pointless.

COVID-19 crashed into our lives with enough force to dislodge most of us from the center of our own universes. It asked us to consider others, our impact, and the futility of our individual success and happiness in the context of other people's suffering. But a generation of nihilists had already discovered this long before they heard of the pandemic. Just as many millennials have been crushed by ideas of meaning, so have others been freed and soothed by embracing nihilism.

Those of us who grew up amid the crumbling ruins of systems that were supposed to reinforce a sense of purpose have developed a unique perspective on our own comfort. We understand that even if we were able to locate meaning within our lives, it would exist inside structures that still largely exploit and ignore so many others. Rather than continue to perpetuate fading myths of individual greatness, a new generation considers the alternative. One that has welcomed into the mainstream ideas of socialized medicine, universal income, sweeping environmental reforms, and the abolition of billionaires. Sunny nihilists aren't defined by a sense of destructive hopelessness, but instead inspired by the idea that individual purpose is a mirage if everyone else around you is living in a desert.

When you look at the things you're supposed to want—a perfect partner, a job people are jealous of, a comprehension of religion—and consider that they and the meaning within them are constructed fantasies, they suddenly seem hollow. They're exposed as institutions that control and coddle us. But when you turn the same attention to what in reality does make you happy—loved ones, nature, a quiet afternoon—they retain all their luster without having myths of purpose mapped over them. A generation that has seen through the futility of meaningless systems understands this. They begin to prioritize these quieter delights, considering the planet, the well-being of others, and a future where all people are able to shelter in such gentle pleasures.

The truth is, we obsess about life to save ourselves from death. We make the question of meaning impossibly big to balance how impossibly small we are. We inflate ourselves to distract from the reality that being good to others is a lot of work. We wish for a magic rule of happiness because the things we need to do to be happy aren't the things that bring attention, praise, direction, and reassurance. But through considering this version of sunny nihilism, we can induce an alternative state, one that says: *Don't worry about locating the meaning of life*; instead ask: *What is my obsession taking me away from right now? How is it trying to make me think and behave? Where could that energy and focus be better spent?*

Across history we've sought meaning in God, love, work, and ourselves. It's not lost on me that in many ways I'm repeating the same trick with this book. Dedicating tens of thousands of words to the power of pointlessness is in essence just another grasp for meaning. Understandably, humans find it impossible to abandon the idea altogether. But that doesn't mean we need to be swallowed by it.

A reality devoid of *any* shade of meaning is difficult to imagine. But sunny nihilism offers an existence that at least isn't consumed by it. It invites us to resist the urge to dress up the actuality of our own lives, blur the existential insanity of existence, the cacophony of mutations that occurred over billions of years to bring us here. Fully embracing the surreal miracle of our lives makes it easier to resist asking too much more from them. The danger of meaning is that it can condition us to feel dissatisfied with the absurd beauty of existence, to endlessly ask "is this it?"

Sunny nihilism reminds us that this is, unavoidably, it. Our lives are a meaningless twist of chance, a bundle of luck and random events. But to exist, to have been able to experience a moment of this pointless planet, feels like such a bizarre gift, it requires no point at all.

ENDNOTES

6: *He who has a why*: Viktor Emil Frankl, *Man's Search for Meaning* (India: Better Yourself Books, 2003), 72.

21: *exploited by the aristocracy*: Kristian Petrov, "'Strike Out, Right and Left!': A Conceptual-Historical Analysis of 1860s Russian Nihilism and Its Notion of Negation," *Studies in East European Thought* 71 (2019): 73–97.

23: *needles in supermarket strawberries*: Kristian Silva, Ellie Sibson, and staff, "Strawberry needle contamination: Accused woman motivated by spite, court hears," ABC News, Australia, November 12, 2018, https://www.abc.net.au/news/2018-11-12/strawberry-needle -contamination-woman-to-face-court/10486770.

24: *Australian fruit industry*: Ben Smee, "The Needles and the Damage Done: the Growers Hurt by Australia's Strawberry Saboteurs," *Guardian*, Australia, September 22, 2018, https://www.theguardian .com/australia-news/2018/sep/22/the-needles-and-the-damage -done-the-growers-hurt-by-australias-strawberry-saboteurs.

24: *The hashtag #smashastrawb*: ABC News Breakfast. "#SmashaStrawb: Social Media Lights Up with Inventive Strawberry Recipes," ABC News, Australia, September 19, 2018, https://www.abc.net.au /news/2018-09-19/social-media-shares-strawberry-recipes-after -needle-scare/10280260.

24: *assistance package for the strawberry industry*: ABC Rural, "Strawberry Needle Contamination: Industry to Get $1m Federal Government Assistance Package," ABC News, Australia, September 19, 2018, https://www.abc.net.au/news/2018-09-19/strawberry-farmers-to -get-federal-government-1-million-dollars/10280682a.

24: *unsubstantiated internet claims*: "Strawberry Needle: Copycat Case Prompts Warning from Authorities to Cut Up Fruit," ABC News, Australia, September 17, 2018, https://www.abc.net.au/news/2018 -09-13/strawberry-recall-needle-found-in-fruit/10240956.

25: *supervisor who acted out of spite*: "Strawberry Needle Contamination: Accused Woman Motivated by Spite, Court Hears"

25: *six counts of contamination of goods*: Cheryl Goodenough, "Strawberry Needle Case: My Ut Trinh Charged with Contamination of Goods at Berrylicious," news.com.au, Australia, June 15, 2020, https:// www.news.com.au/national/queensland/courts-law/strawberry -needle-case-my-ut-trinh-charged-with-contamination-of-goods -at-berrylicious/news-story/40ae2673397e04e516f896eb10a949d4.

26: *beside streams full of fish*: Earnest Becker, *The Birth and Death of Meaning* (New York: Free Press, 2010), 98.

27: *inherent amorality of nihilism*: Alan Pratt, "Nihilism," *Internet Encyclopedia of Philosophy*. "Alan Pratt." https://iep.utm.edu/nihilism/.

28: *university's 400-year history*: R. Lanier Anderson, "Friedrich Nietzsche," *The Stanford Encyclopedia of Philosophy* (Summer 2017), https://plato .stanford.edu/archives/sum2017/entries/nietzsche.

28: *suffered a mental breakdown*: D. Hemelsoet, K. Hemelsoet, D. Devreese, "The Neurological Illness of Friedrich Nietzsche," *Acta neurologica Belgica* vol. 108,1 (2008): 9–16, https://pubmed.ncbi.nlm.nih .gov/18575181.

28: *fracture in how his ideas*: Sue Prideaux, "Far Right, Misogynist, Humourless? Why Nietzsche Is Misunderstood," *Guardian*, October 6, 2018, https://www.theguardian.com/books/2018/oct/06 /exploding-nietzsche-myths-need-dynamiting.

29: *rebirth of the human race*: Simon Romero, "German Outpost Born of Racism in 1887 Blends Into Paraguay," *New York Times*, May 5, 2013, https://www.nytimes.com/2013/05/06/world/americas/german -outpost-born-of-racism-blends-into-paraguay.html.

29: *mendacious race swindle*: "Far Right, Misogynist, Humourless? Why Nietzsche Is Misunderstood"

30: *nationalism which foments*: Michael F. Duffy and Willard Mittelman, "Nietzsche's Attitudes Toward the Jews," *Journal of the History of Ideas* 49, no. 2 (1988): 301–17. Accessed April 20, 2021. doi:10.2307/2709502.

30: *Nietzsche's intense friendship*: Emrys Westacott, "Why Did Nietzsche Break with Wagner?" ThoughtCo, March 4, 2019, https://www.thoughtco.com/why-did-nietzsche-break-with-wagner-2670457.

31: *mere dress rehearsal*: Friedrich Nietzsche, *The Gay Science: With a Prelude in Rhymes and an Appendix of Songs* (New York: Vintage Books, 1974), 286.

32: *faith in reason in life*: Simon May, *Nietzsche on Freedom and Autonomy* (Oxford: Oxford University Press, 2009), 25.

35: *parks banning screaming*: Austin Horn, "'Please Scream Inside Your Heart,' Japanese Amusement Park Tells Thrill-Seekers," NPR, July 9, 2020, https://www.npr.org/sections/coronavirus-live-updates/2020/07/09/889394605/please-scream-inside-your-heart-japanese-amusement-park-tells-thrill-seekers.

36: *Celebrities to Kill You*: Jia Tolentino, "Love, Death, and Begging for Celebrities to Kill You." *New Yorker*, June 21, 2019, https://www.newyorker.com/culture/cultural-comment/love-death-and-begging-for-celebrities-to-kill-you.

37: *Run Them Over*: Gabriella Paiella, "Why Does Everyone Want Their Crushes to Run Them Over?," *The Cut*, January 10, 2019, https://www.thecut.com/2019/01/people-tweeting-run-me-over-at-celebrities.html.

38: *do extreme damage*: Nosheen Iqbal, "'I Want to Do Extreme Damage': Harmony Korine's Third Coming," *Guardian*, February 24, 2016, https://www.theguardian.com/film/2016/feb/24/harmony-korines-art-rehab.

39: *more of a horror film*: Manohla Dargis, "Debauchery and the American Experience (Woo-Hoo!)," *New York Times*, March 14, 2013, https://www.nytimes.com/2013/03/15/movies/spring-breakers-directed-by-harmony-korine.html.

39: *dimension truly matters*: Hazem Fahmy, "SXSW 2019 Review: The Beach Bum: McConaughey Embarks on Booze-soaked Journey of Cheerful Nihilism," *Film Inquiry*, March 11, 2019, https://www.film inquiry.com/sxsw-beach-bum-2019-review/.

41: *simply no true world*: *The Oxford Handbook of Philosophy in Music Education* (Oxford: Oxford University Press, 2012), 391.

41: *has an existential crisis*: *The Good Place*, Season 3, Episode 5, "Jeremy Bearimy," written by Megan Amram, aired October 18, 2018, on NBC.

43: *devastating Atlantic article*: Annie Lowrey, "Millennials Don't Stand a Chance," *Atlantic*, April 13, 2020, https://www.theatlantic.com /ideas/archive/2020/04/millennials-are-new-lost-generation /609832/.

44: *like a societal collapse*: Ryan Brooks, "Generation Freefall," *BuzzFeed News*, April 20, 2020, https://www.buzzfeednews.com/article /ryancbrooks/gen-z-young-millennials-coronavirus-pandemic-recession.

45: *an incomprehensible world*: Joseph Dillier, "Ironic Nihilism: Our Generation's Best Creation," *The Daily Illini*, February 23, 2019, https://dailyillini.com/opinions/2019/02/23/ironic-nihilism-our-generations-best-creation/.

45: *the musician Kesha*: Jael Goldfine, "Don't Cry for Kesha," *Paper*, February 20, 2020, https://www.papermag.com/kesha-high-road-2645194946.html?rebelltitem=2#rebelltitem2.

47: *Gladwell explores how*: Malcolm Gladwell, "Hamlet Was Wrong," *Revisionist History* (podcast), August 2020, https://www.pushkin .fm/episode/hamlet-was-wrong/.

52: *their future plummeting*: Ryan Brooks, "Generation Freefall," *BuzzFeed News*, April 20, 2020, https://www.buzzfeednews.com/article /ryancbrooks/gen-z-young-millennials-coronavirus-pandemic -recession.

53: *save that future*: Greta Thunberg, "I'm Striking from School to Protest Inaction on Climate Change—You Should Too," *Guardian*, November 27, 2018, https://www.theguardian.com/commentis-free/2018/nov/26/im-striking-from-school-for-climate-change-too-save-the-world-australians-students-should-too.

53: *even the dog*: Emily Witt, "How Greta Thunberg Transformed Existential Dread into a Movement," *New Yorker*, April 6, 2020, https://www.newyorker.com/books/under-review/how-greta -thunberg-transformed-existential-dread-into-a-movement.

53: *her insistence on pessimism*: Emily Witt, "How Greta Thunberg Transformed Existential Dread into a Movement"

56: *less government support*: ABC staff, "Lockdown of Victoria's Public Housing Towers During COVID Crisis Breached Human Rights, Ombudsman Finds," ABC News, December 17, 2020, https://www .abc.net.au/news/2020-12-17/lockdown-public-housing-towers -breached-human-rights-ombudsman/12991162.

56: *mutual aid groups*: Rachel Conaghan, "Here's How You Can Help Those Stuck in Victoria's Public Housing Towers," *Junkee*, July 7, 2020, https://junkee.com/donations-melbourne-public-housing/260770.

63: *the Burnout Generation*: Anne Helen Peterson, "How Millennials Became the Burnout Generation," *BuzzFeed News*, January 5, 2019, https://www.buzzfeednews.com/article/annehelenpetersen /millennials-burnout-generation-debt-work.

65: *technologies we use daily:* Jenny Odell, *How to Do Nothing: Resisting the Attention Economy* (Brooklyn: Melville House, 2019), ix.

68: *allegations of toxic work culture*: Anonymous, "Hell Is Working at the Huffington Post," *Gawker*, June 2, 2015, http://tktk.gawker.com /hell-is-working-at-the-huffington-post-1707724052.

68: *contributors and being*: William D. Cohan, "The Inside Story of Why Arianna Huffington Left the Huffington Post," *Vanity Fair*, September 8, 2016, https://www.vanityfair.com/news/2016/09/why -arianna-huffington-left-the-huffington-post.

68: *news media at large*: The Editors. "Aggregated Robbery," *New Republic*, March 3, 2011, https://newrepublic.com/article/84509 /huffington-post-aggregation-google.

70: *discussed and criticized*: Apple, "The Whole Working-from-home Thing," July 14, 2020, *YouTube* video, 6:55, https://www.youtube .com/watch?v=6_pru8U2RmM&t=4s.

73: *(often shoplifted) vintage*: Ariana Romero, "All the Items Sophia Steals in Girlboss," *Refinery29*, April 26, 2017, https://www.refinery29.com /en-us/2017/04/151522/girlboss-sophia-shoplifting-stolen-items.

73: *working for the Man*: Amoruso Sophia, *#GIRLBOSS* (New York: Portfolio/Penguin, 2014), 94.

73: *women in the world*: Clare O'Connor, "Nasty Gal's Sophia Amoruso Hits Richest Self-Made Women List with $280 Million Fortune," *Forbes*, June 1, 2016, https://www.forbes.com/sites/clareoconnor /2016/06/01/nasty-gal-sophia-amoruso-richest-women-net-worth /?sh=42fbf7915774.

73: *file for bankruptcy*: Samantha Sharf, "What Sophia Amoruso Learned from Nasty Gal's Bankruptcy," *Forbes*, October 3, 2017, https:// www.forbes.com/sites/samanthasharf/2017/10/03/what-sophia -amoruso-learned-from-nasty-gals-bankruptcy/?sh=318c59694523.

73: *go on maternity leave*: Valeriya Safronova, "Nasty Gal's Path to Bankruptcy," *New York Times*, November 11, 2016, https://www .nytimes.com/2016/11/11/fashion/nasty-gal-sophia-amoruso -bankruptcy.html.

73: *a kind of alchemy*: Sophia Amoruso, *#GIRLBOSS*, 28.

74: *companies like Thinx*: Hilary George-Parkin, "Thinx Promised a Feminist Utopia to Everyone but Its Employees," *Vox*, March 14, 2017, https://www.vox.com/2017/3/14/14911228/thinx-miki-agrawal -health-care-branding.

74: *Away*: Zoe Schiffer, "Emotional Baggage," *The Verge*, December 5, 2019, https://www.theverge.com/2019/12/5/20995453/away-luggage -ceo-steph-korey-toxic-work-environment-travel-inclusion.

74: *Outdoor Voices*: Brianna Sacks, "Outdoor Voices Became a Staple for Millennial Cool Girls Thanks to Its Chill Aesthetic. Employees Say They Were Drowning," *BuzzFeed News*, March 11, 2020, https:// www.buzzfeednews.com/article/briannasacks/outdoor-voices -ty-haney-employee-allegations.

74: *and the Wing*: Amanda Hess, "The Wing Is a Women's Utopia. Unless You Work There," *New York Times*, March 17, 2020, https://www .nytimes.com/2020/03/17/magazine/the-wing.html.

74: *the most infamous*: Walter Kirn, "The Cautionary Tale of Adam Neumann and WeWork," *New York Times*, October 23, 2020, https://www.nytimes.com/2020/10/23/books/review/billion -dollar-loser-adam-neumann-wework-reeves-wiedeman.html https://www.nytimes.com/2020/03/17/magazine/the-wing.html.

75: *thousands of employees*: Dominic Rushe, "WeWork Announces 2,400 Employees to Lose Their Jobs." *Guardian*, November 22, 2019, https://www.theguardian.com/business/2019/nov/21/we-work -job-losses-layoffs-global-adam-neumann.

75: *hundreds of millions of dollars*: Grace Dean, "Adam Neumann Will Reportedly Leave WeWork's Board for a Year as Part of His SoftBank Settlement—and Take Home an Extra $50 Million Payout," *Business Insider, Australia*, February 25, 2021, https://www.businessinsider. com.au/softbank-wework-stock-adam-neumann-board-payout -wework-ipo-settlement-2021-2.

75: *she reflects on the unique*: Leigh Stein, "The End of the Girlboss Is Here," *Medium*, June 23, 2020, https://gen.medium.com/the-end -of-the-girlboss-is-nigh-4591dec34ed8.

81: *the very talented*: Julian Morgans, "Maybe Your Big Dream Is Making You Unhappy," *VICE*, May 22, 2020, https://www.vice.com/en/arti- cle/y3zg9b/maybe-your-big-dream-life-goal-ambition-is-making -you-unhappy.

87: *fused together by love*: K. Scarlett Kingsley and Richard Parry, "Empedocles," *The Stanford Encyclopedia of Philosophy,* Summer 2020, Edward N. Zalta (ed.), https://plato.stanford.edu/archives /sum2020/entries/empedocles/.

87: *parable of predestined love*: Firmin DeBrander, "What Plato can teach you about finding a soulmate," *The Conversation*, February 14, 2017, https://theconversation.com/what-plato-can-teach-you-about -finding-a-soulmate-72715.

87: *halved for pickling*: *The Dialogues of Plato* (Oxford: Clarendon Press, 1875), 41.

90: *a great beautifier*: Louisa May Alcott, *Little Women, or Meg, Jo, Beth, and Amy: Parts I and II* (Boston: Roberts Brothers, 1880), 260.

90: *rather than chaotic*: Clemency Pleming, "Did Love Begin in the Middle Ages?" *Oxford Arts Blog*, August 14, 2014, https://www .ox.ac.uk/news/arts-blog/did-love-begin-middle-ages.

91: *heard there was such a thing*: "La Rochefoucauld," *The School of Life*, https://www.theschooloflife.com/thebookoflife/the-great -philosophers-la-rochefoucauld/.

91: *being in romantic love*: V. Karandashev, "A Cultural Perspective on Romantic Love," *Online Readings in Psychology and Culture*, June 2015, https://doi.org/10.9707/2307-0919.1135.

92: *love's reputation a little*: The School of Life, "History of Ideas—Love," August 7, 2015, *YouTube* video, 15:23, https://www.youtube.com /watch?v=fK2IJ43ppd0.

95: *to sell nylons*: *Mad Men*, Season 1, Episode 1, "Smoke Gets in Your Eyes," written by Matthew Weiner, aired July 19, 2007, on HBO.

96: *relationship is normative*: Elizabeth Brake, *Minimizing Marriage: Marriage, Morality, and the Law* (Oxford: Oxford University Press, 2012), Chapter 4.iii.

97: *Looking at the happiness levels*: Paul Dolan, *Happy Ever After: Escaping the Myth of the Perfect Life* (London: Penguin Books Limited, 2019), X.

97: *live a little longer*: Sian Cain, "Women Are Happier Without Children or a Spouse, Says Happiness Expert," *Guardian*, May 25, 2019, https://www.theguardian.com/lifeandstyle/2019/may/25/women -happier-without-children-or-a-spouse-happiness-expert.

98: *focus, and motivation*: Bonnie Christian, "What Is Love? Science Kinda Has the Answer," *WIRED*, August 7, 2017, https://www.wired .co.uk/article/what-is-love.

99: *for twenty seconds*: Arthur C. Brooks, "Opinion: How Social Distancing Could Ultimately Teach Us How to Be Less Lonely," *Washington Post*, March 21, 2020, https://www.washingtonpost .com/opinions/how-social-distancing-could-ultimately-teach-us -how-to-be-less-lonely/2020/03/20/ca459804-694e-11ea-9923 -57073adce27c_story.html.

99: *Brooks looked back*: Arthur C. Brooks, "Love Is Medicine for Fear," *Atlantic*, July 16, 2020, https://www.theatlantic.com/family/archive /2020/07/how-fight-fear-love/614227/.

99: *German philosopher Arthur*: Arthur Schopenhauer, *The World as Will and Representation, Vol. 1.* (Mineola, NY: Dover Publications, 2012), X.

103: *her 1949 exploration*: Simone de Beauvoir, *The Second Sex*, trans. Howard Madison Parshley (New York: Vintage Books, 1997), X.

109: *he observed that a belief*: Charles Darwin, *The Descent of Man and Selection in Relation to Sex* (New York: Appleton and Co., 1883), 7, 609, 612–614, 618–619.

110: *psychologist Jesse Bering*: Robin Marantz Henig, "Darwin's God," *New York Times*, March 4, 2007, https://www.nytimes.com/2007/03/04 /magazine/04evolution.t.html.

110: *underlying psychological propensity*: Richard Dawkins, *The God Delusion* (London: Black Swan, 2006), 202.

111: *reporting on their efforts*: Liat Clark, "Believing in God can trigger the same reward regions of the brain as taking drugs," *WIRED*, November 30, 2016, https://www.wired.co.uk/article/mormons -experience-religion-like-drug-takers-feel-highs-neuroscientists -say.

112: *becomes neurologically real*: Brandon Ambrosino, "Do humans have a 'religion instinct'?" BBC, May 30, 2019, https://www.bbc.com /future/article/20190529-do-humans-have-a-religion-instinct.

114: *through our elevation of science*: Friedrich Nietzsche, *The Gay Science: With a Prelude in Rhymes and an Appendix of Songs* (New York: Vintage Books, 1974), 181.

114: *Americans said they belonged*: Jeffery M. Jones, "U.S. Church Membership Falls Below Majority for First Time," *Gallup*, March 29, 2021, https://news.gallup.com/poll/341963/church-membership -falls-below-majority-first-time.aspx.

114: *ironically that makes them*: Robert P. Jones, Daniel Cox, Betsy Cooper, and Rachel Lienesch, "Exodus: Why Americans Are Leaving Religion—and Why They're Unlikely to Come Back," *PRRI*, 2016, http://www.prri.org/research/prri-rns-poll-nones-atheist-leaving -religion/.

114: *affiliated with any faith*: "In U.S., Decline of Christianity Continues at Rapid Pace," *Pew Research Center*, October 17, 2019, https:// www.pewforum.org/2019/10/17/in-u-s-decline-of-christianity -continues-at-rapid-pace/.

115: *prerequisite for a moral life*: Daniel Cox, Amelia Thomson-DeVeaux, "Millennials Are Leaving Religion and Not Coming Back," *FiveThirtyEight*, December 12, 2019, https://fivethirtyeight.com /features/millennials-are-leaving-religion-and-not-coming -back/.

115: *resistant to peer pressure*: Deena Prichep, "Teaching Children to Ask the Big Questions Without Religion," NPR, June 16, 2018, https://www.npr.org/2018/06/16/618217795/teaching-children-to -ask-the-big-questions-without-religion.

118: *four trillion dollars*: Eric Rosenbaum, "The job benefit that can help lower your rising health insurance payroll deduction," CNBC, April 1, 2019, https://www.cnbc.com/2019/04/01/the-job-benefit -that-can-lower-your-health-insurance-payroll-deduction.html.

118: *economic growth in general*: "2018 Global Wellness Economy Monitor," *Global Wellness Institute*, Miami, 2018. April 25, 2021, https://globalwellnessinstitute.org/industry-research/2018-global -wellness-economy-monitor/.

119: *can be incredibly attractive*: Kari Paul, "Why Millennials Are Ditching Religion for Witchcraft and Astrology," *MarketWatch*, October 31, 2018, https://www.marketwatch.com/story/why-millennials-are -ditching-religion-for-witchcraft-and-astrology-2017-10-20.

120: *fully explainable by science*: Claire Comstock-Gay, "Who Cares If Astrology Isn't 'Real'? It's Not a Science—Which Is Why I Love It." *The Cut*, May 14, 2020, https://www.thecut.com/2020/05/book -excerpt-madame-clairevoyants-guide-to-the-stars.html.

121: *three million times*: Paige Leskin, "Millennials Are Bringing Astrology Back Into the Mainstream with This Popular iPhone App—Here's How to Use Co-Star to See Who You're Compatible with," *Business Insider*, April 18, 2019, https://www.businessinsider.com/co-star -iphone-app-popular-with-millennials-is-bringing-astrology-back -2019-4?r=AU&IR=T.

121: *history and the universe*: Kari Paul, "Millennials Are Ditching Religion for Astrology," *New York Post*, October 23, 2017, https://nypost .com/2017/10/23/millennials-are-ditching-religion-for-astrology/.

122: *mega-church extravaganza*: Amanda Mull, "I Joined a Stationary-Biker Gang," *Atlantic*, December 2019, https://www.theatlantic .com/magazine/archive/2019/12/the-tribe-of-peloton/600748/.

122: *quoted as calling the program*: Olivia Petter, "The Cult of Peloton: How an At-Home Spinning Community Became a Pandemic Obsession," *Independent*, November 27, 2020, https://www.independent .co.uk/life-style/peloton-lockdown-instructors-change-lives -b1759232.html.

123: *may experience better health*: Joey Marshal, "Are Religious People Happier, Healthier? Our New Global Study Explores This Question," *Pew Research Center*, January 31, 2019, https://pewrsr.ch /2MEWOYx.

124: *Oprah to step in*: David Atkins, "Oprah for President?" *Rolling Stone*, January 9, 2018, https://www.rollingstone.com/politics /politics-features/oprah-for-president-121888/.

130: *gazes also into you*: Friedrich Nietzsche, *Beyond Good & Evil: Prelude to a Philosophy of the Future* (New York: Vintage Books, 2010), 89.

134: *philosophized with a hammer*: Friedrich Nietzsche, *Twilight of the Idols: How to Philosophize with a Hammer* (N.P.: CreateSpace Independent Publishing Platform, 2016), X.

134: *The Alt-Right Is Drunk*: Sean Illing, "The Alt-Right Is Drunk on Bad Readings of Nietzsche. The Nazis Were Too," *Vox*, December 30, 2018, https://www.vox.com/2017/8/17/16140846/alt-right-nietzsche -richard-spencer-nazism.

135: *a blessing to mankind*: Sue Prideaux, "Far Right, Misogynist, Humourless? Why Nietzsche Is Misunderstood," *Guardian*,

October 6, 2018, https://www.theguardian.com/books/2018/oct/06/exploding-nietzsche-myths-need-dynamiting.

137: *broadly breaking down*: Kevin Roose, "What Is QAnon, the Viral Pro-Trump Conspiracy Theory?" *New York Times*, March 4, 2021, https://www.nytimes.com/article/what-is-qanon.html.

137: *followers have been linked*: Lois Becket, "QAnon: A Timeline of Violence Linked to the Conspiracy Theory," *Guardian*, October 16, 2020, https://www.theguardian.com/us-news/2020/oct/15/qanon-violence-crimes-timeline.

137: *conspiracy theory-driven domestic extremists*: Jana Winter, "Exclusive: FBI Document Warns Conspiracy Theories Are a New Domestic Terrorism Threat," *Yahoo! News*, August 2, 2019, https://news.yahoo.com/fbi-documents-conspiracy-theories-terrorism-160000507.html.

138: *Georgia's Fourteenth Congressional District*: Sam Levin, "QAnon Supporter Marjorie Taylor Greene Wins Seat in US House," *Guardian*, November 4, 2020, https://www.theguardian.com/us-news/2020/nov/03/qanon-marjorie-taylor-greene-wins-congress.

139: *barricades of civilization*: Richard Hofstadter, "The Paranoid Style in American Politics," *Harper's Magazine*, November 1964, https://harpers.org/archive/1964/11/the-paranoid-style-in-american-politics/.

139: *what's going on around them*: Oliver Gordon, "Under Financial Pressure and Slipping into Conspiracies, Why Instagram Influencers Promote Coronavirus Lockdown Protests," ABC News, May 17, 2020, https://www.abc.net.au/news/2020-05-15/why-instagram-influencers-are-drawn-to-coronavirus-conspiracies/12250152.

140: *deep the rabbit hole goes*: *The Matrix*, directed by Lana Wachowski and Lilly Wachowski (Warner Bros., 1999).

141: *men's rights movements*: Stephen Marche, "Swallowing the Red Pill: a Journey to the Heart of Modern Misogyny," *Guardian*, April 14, 2016, https://www.theguardian.com/technology/2016/apr/14/the-red-pill-reddit-modern-misogyny-manosphere-men.

142: *Men and Mental Health*: Aja Romano, "What a Woman-led Incel Support Group Can Teach Us About Men and Mental Health," *Vox*, June 20, 2018, https://www.vox.com/2018/6/20/17314846/incel -support-group-therapy-black-pill-mental-health.

142: *a chilling reference*: Zack Beauchamp, "Our Incel Problem," *Vox*, April 23, 2019, https://www.vox.com/the-highlight/2019/4/16/18287446 /incel-definition-reddit.

142: *dark hero figure*: "Elliot Rodger: How Misogynist Killer Became 'Incel Hero,'" BBC, April 16, 2018, https://www.bbc.com/news /world-us-canada-43892189.

142: *in his Atlantic article*: Jeffery Goldberg, "The Conspiracy Theorists Are Winning," *Atlantic*, May 13, 2020, https://www.theatlantic .com/ideas/archive/2020/05/shadowland-introduction/610840/.

143: *turn people gay*: Tucker Higgins, "Alex Jones' 5 Most Disturbing and Ridiculous Conspiracy Theories," CNBC, September 15, 2018, https://www.cnbc.com/2018/09/14/alex-jones-5-most-disturbing -ridiculous-conspiracy-theories.html.

143: *$20 million a year*: Elizabeth Williamson, Emily Steel, "Conspiracy Theories Made Alex Jones Very Rich. They May Bring Him Down." *New York Times*, September 7, 2018, https://www.nytimes .com/2018/09/07/us/politics/alex-jones-business-infowars -conspiracy.html.

144: *suffering of their children*: David Benatar, *Better Never to Have Been* (Oxford: Clarendon Press, 2008), 6.

145: *gratuitous and unbearable*: Joshua Rothman, "The Case for Not Being Born," *New Yorker*, November 27, 2017, https://www.newyorker .com/culture/persons-of-interest/the-case-for-not-being-born.

149: *closest to them seem insignificant*: Chris Jones, "The Woman Who Might Find Us Another Earth," *New York Times*, December 7, 2016, https://www.nytimes.com/2016/12/07/magazine/the-world-sees -me-as-the-one-who-will-find-another-earth.html.

153: *young people compete*: Richard Layard, "How to Make the World Happier—and Why It Should Be Our First Priority," *Guardian*, January 19, 2020, https://www.theguardian.com/books/2020

/jan/19/why-world-needs-new-politics-happiness-can-we-be
-happier-evidence-and-ethics-richard-layard.

154: *people dying in Africa*: Uptini Saiidi, "Why Mark Zuckerberg's New Year
Resolution Is His Most Important One Yet," CNBC, January 10, 2017,
https://www.cnbc.com/2017/01/10/why-mark-zuckerbergs-new
-year-resolution-is-his-most-important-one-yet.html.

154: *mold of their own devising*: Zadie Smith, *Intimations: Six Essays* (New
York: Penguin Books, 2020), 4.

157: *none of these finally satisfy*: Walt Whitman, *Specimen Days and Collect*
(Philadelphia: David McKay, 1883), 82.

159: *become a universal law*: Robert Johnson and Adam Cureton, "Kant's
Moral Philosophy," *The Stanford Encyclopedia of Philosophy* (Spring
2021), Edward N. Zalta (ed.), https://plato.stanford.edu/archives
/spr2021/entries/kant-moral/.

160: *all the ordinary divides*: Rebecca Solnit, *A Paradise Built in Hell: The
Extraordinary Communities That Arise in Disaster* (New York: Viking
Penguin, 2010), 3.

163: *instead, he urged readers*: *Radical Love: Teachings from the Islamic
Mystical Tradition*, trans. Omid Safi (New Haven: Yale University
Press, 2018), 256.

163: *he reflected on the poet*: Sigal Samuel, "What Would Rumi Do in a
Pandemic?" *Future Perfect*, July 15, 2020, https://www.vox.com
/future-perfect/2020/7/15/21315120/rumi-sufism-muslim-pandemic
-isolation-omid-safi.

164: *earth-quaking essay*: Wendy Syfret, "The Cultural Insights of Jia
Tolentino," *The Saturday Paper*, October 19, 2019, https://www
.thesaturdaypaper.com.au/culture/books/2019/10/19/the-cultural
-insights-jia-tolentino/15714036008958#hrd.

168: *Buddhist teacher Dr. Nikki*: Sigal Samuel, "The Surprising Benefits
of Contemplating Your Death," *Future Perfect*, August 12, 2020.
https://www.vox.com/21363483/mindfulness-of-death-mortality
-meditation-nikki-mirghafori.

170: *happening to us right now*: David Konstan, "Epicurus," *The Stanford
Encyclopedia of Philosophy* (Summer 2018), Edward N. Zalta (ed.),
https://plato.stanford.edu/archives/sum2018/entries/epicurus.

171: *raising a very ill child*: Heather Lanier, "Surrendering to Uncertainty," *Atlantic*, May 16, 2020, https://www.theatlantic.com/ideas/archive /2020/05/surrendering-uncertainty/611446/.

172: *better and emptier you feel*: Deborah Wye, *Artists and Prints: Masterworks from The Museum of Modern Art* (New York: Museum of Modern Art, 2004), 162. https://www.moma.org/collection /works/61240.

174: *possible lives sound heroic*: Staff writers, "Coronavirus Will Change the World Permanently. Here's How." *Politico*, March 19, 2020, https:// www.politico.com/news/magazine/2020/03/19/coronavirus -effect-economy-life-society-analysis-covid-135579.

ACKNOWLEDGMENTS

T his book was written on the land of the Wurundjeri people of the Kulin Nation. I want to acknowledge them as the traditional custodians and pay my respects to their Elders past and present. As well as recognize their continuing culture and the contribution they make to the city where I live. The work and activism of Aboriginal and Torres Strait Islander individuals influenced many of this project's themes. Specifically, how we consider our place in history, and our responsibility for this fragile, beautiful planet. If you are a non-Indigenous person reading this, I really encourage you to look into how you can support First Nations individuals by Paying the Rent in your own life.

My formal journey with sunny nihilism began with a *Guardian* article I wrote under the care of Alyx Gorman. I'll forever be grateful for her confidence in me and the idea. The evolution of sunny nihilism into a book would not have been possible without my agent Rachel Mills, who (I don't feel it's an exaggeration to say) changed my life.

The majority of this project came together while I was living through rolling COVID-19 lockdowns. Many times I felt like the book, and the gentle and thoughtful guidance of my editor Cindy Chan, were the only things holding my fraying brain together. Writing a book during a global pandemic is (not surprisingly) complex, which is why I'll always be grateful to Cara Bedick for her help in imagining how this book will exist now and into the future. She's that magical kind of editor who makes you feel confident enough to believe you can do better.

While my journey with sunny nihilism began in 2019, it was the product of my family's lifelong dedication to discussion, debate, and exploration. I can't comprehend my luck of being part of such a brilliant congregation. Ben, Margie, Tony, Gill, Dan, Dave, Katie, Mitch, I love you more than I can bear.

Finally, I want to (again) thank my partner Ben and my mother Margie. Both of whom directly inspired huge sections of this book and spent countless hours unpicking ideas and concepts with me—even when they didn't always agree.

BEN THOMSON

ABOUT THE AUTHOR

Wendy Syfret is an award-winning Melbourne-based writer, editor, and author whose work has appeared in *VICE, i-D,* and the *Guardian.* Her first book, *How to Think Like an Activist,* was published in 2020. Formerly managing editor for *VICE Asia* and head of editorial for *VICE Australia,* she now works freelance and tries not to take everything too seriously.